The

WAGE
Carrot
and the
PENSION
Stick

RETIREMENT BENEFITS	and	**LABOR FORCE PARTICIPATION**

Laurence J. Kotlikoff
David A. Wise

1989

W. E. UPJOHN INSTITUTE for Employment Research
Kalamazoo, Michigan

Library of Congress Cataloging-in-Publication Data

Kotlikoff, Laurence J.
   The wage carrot and the pension stick : retirement benefits and
labor force participation / Laurence J. Kotlikoff, David A. Wise.
      p.   cm.
   Includes bibliographical references.
   ISBN 0-88099-082-1. — ISBN 0-88099-081-3 (pbk.)
   1. Old age pensions—United States.   2. Retirement age—United
States.   3. Age and employment—United States.   I. Wise, David A.
II. Rirlw.
HD7105.35.U6K68   1989
331.25'2'0973—dc20   ∞   89-39488
                                                              CIP

Materials in chapters 2, 3, and 4 of this volume are from:

Kotlikoff and Wise, "Labor Compensation and the Structure of Private Pension Plans: Evidence for Contractual Versus Spot Labor Markets," appearing in PENSIONS, LABOR, AND INDIVIDUAL CHOICE, ed. by Wise, University of Chicago Press, (1985): 55-87

   (© 1985 by the National Bureau of Economic Research. All rights reserved.)

Kotlikoff and Wise, "The Incentive Effects of Private Pension Plans," appearing in ISSUES IN PENSION ECONOMICS, ed. by Zvi Bodie, John Shoven, and David Wise, University of Chicago Press (1987): 283-336

   (© 1987 by the National Bureau of Economic Research. All rights reserved.)

To Dayle and Madeline.

THE AUTHORS

Laurence J. Kotlikoff is Chairman of the Department of Economics at Boston University and a Research Associate of the National Bureau of Economic Research. He received his Ph.D. in Economics from Harvard University in 1977 and subsequently taught at the University of California, Los Angeles and at Yale University. In 1981-82 he served as a Senior Economist with the President's Council of Economic Advisers. He is author of *What Dertermines Savings?*, co-author (with Alan Auerbach) of *Dynamic Fiscal Policy,* and co-author (with Daniel Smith) of *Pensions in the American Economy,* and has published many articles on issues of deficits and the tax structure, social security, pensions, saving, and insurance.

David A. Wise is John F. Stambaugh Professor of Political Economy in the John F. Kennedy School of Government, Harvard University. He received his Ph.D. in Economics from the University of California, Berkeley in 1973. He is a Research Associate and Program Director at The National Bureau of Economic Research and serves on the Board of Editors of the *Journal of Labor Economics.* Professor Wise is the editor of *Economics of Aging,* co-editor of *Pensions in the U.S. Economy* and *Issues in Pension Economics,* and contributor to numerous books and journals.

EXECUTIVE SUMMARY

Notwithstanding the Employee Retirement Income Security Act of 1974, many defined benefit pension plans continue to backload severely the accrual of their workers' pension benefits. This backloading no longer takes the form of long service requirements for vesting; rather it is achieved through the use of early retirement benefit reduction provisions and early retirement supplemental benefits. These features produce, in many cases, the same effect as pre-ERISA vesting requirements, namely, that workers who leave employment, whether voluntarily or involuntarily, prior to a specified age or prior to having a specified amount of service, may leave with quite small pension benefits.

In addition to backloading their pension benefits, many firms appear to use their pensions to provide major incentives for workers to leave the firm after a specified age or amount of service. These retirement incentives (old age work disincentives) are often quite large when compared with social security's old age work disincentives. The pension thus becomes, for older workers, the stick to get them to retire and thereby give up the wage carrot.

This monograph documents the continued backloading of pension benefits and the extent of retirement incentives by examining pension accrual in a large sample of U.S. defined benefit pension plans and in one large Fortune 500 firm. In the case of the large Fortune 500 firm, it is possible to link the retirement behavior of workers to the retirement incentives associated with the firm's pension plan.

The monograph begins by defining pension accrual and describing the factors that influence this form of employee compensation. In so doing, it points out the remarkable variety in pension accrual that can arise because of differences in pension provisions and economic circumstances such as the growth rate of employee wages or the interest rate. Pension accrual may not only differ greatly across firms because of differences in pension plans and across time because of differences in economic circumstances, but also across workers within a firm who have different amounts of service, different mortality probabilities, and are of different ages.

While pension accrual is typically a small component of total employee compensation, at some ages and depending on the pension plan, it can easily represent as much as one-half to two-thirds of total compensation. At certain ages it can also reduce total compensation by such magnitudes. The fact that large changes occur from one year to the next in a worker's pension accrual without a concommitant offsetting change in nonpension compensation indicates that the labor market cannot be viewed as clearing on an annual basis; i.e., the size of pension accrual rules out the possibility that workers are paid each year

v

what they produce that year. In ruling out such an annual spot market view of the labor market, the data appear to rule in the only alternative view, namely, that the labor market clears on a long-term implicit contractual basis.

In addition to telling us something about the nature of labor markets, the large magnitudes of pension accrual at specific ages suggests the need for employers to track carefully the pension benefits accruing to each worker. As the appendicies to the monograph show, such tracking requires careful actuarial calculations that are sensitive to the fine details of the pension plan.

The monograph reports the results of such painstaking actuarial calculations for over 1500 U.S. defined benefit plans. These calculations indicate that many plans exhibit significant backloading and most plans generate substantial retirement incentives, often at the plan's age of early retirement. The extent of backloading and retirement incentives differs widely across firms. While there are some differences, on average, in backloading and retirement incentives across industries and occupations, these differences are due primarily to different choices of early and normal retirement ages. For example, early and normal retirement at age 55 is quite common among firms in the transportation industry, and accounts for most of the differences, on average, between pension accrual in transportation and other industries such as manufacturing.

The analysis of the retirement response to the large Fortune 500 company's pension plan yields quite strong findings. The plan is highly backoaded, with most of the benefits accruing in the year the worker reaches age 55, the plan's age of early retirement. The plan also provides a very substantial incentive to retire at age 55 or shortly thereafter; it does so by greatly reducing pension accrual after age 55 and indeed, depending on the worker's service, making pension accrual significantly negative after age 55. The data reveal a very strong retirement response to the plan's retirement incentives. Before workers reach age 55, departure rates are typically around 2 percent. At age 55 they jump to 10 percent or more. Between age 55 and 60 they remain above 10 percent and increase again at age 60. In total, it appears that the pension plan is increasing the extent of early retirement between ages 55 and 60 by roughly one-third.

Given the rapid aging of the U.S. workforce and the growing concern with old age income security, it may be time to take another look at government policy concerning private pension plans. In the absence of new approaches to the retirement incentives of private pensions, government policies designed to increase labor force participation of the elderly by, for example, altering social security may prove highly ineffectual.

ACKNOWLEDGMENTS

We are grateful to The W. E. Upjohn Institute for Employment Research, The National Institute of Aging (grant number 3P01AG05842-01), The Department of Health and Human Services, and The National Bureau of Economic Research for research support. We also wish to thank Steven Woodbury, Robert Spiegelman, Allan Hunt, and an anonymous reviewer for very helpful comments. We are particularly grateful to the vice-president of the large corporation who provided us with data on a confidential basis. Gary Heaton and Jagadeesh Gokhale provided outstanding research assistance.

CONTENTS

LIST OF TABLES

APPENDIX TABLES

LIST OF FIGURES

1
Introduction

Private pensions are playing an increasingly important role in the U.S. economy. Almost half of the U.S. workforce is currently participating in a private, state, or local pension plan, and almost a third of current retirees are recipients of pension benefits. Pension funds hold over 10 percent of U.S. financial assets, and pension liabilities represent a major source of business debt.

Much of the growth in private pensions has occurred in the last three decades. During this period, and especially in the last decade, the labor force participation of older workers had declined dramatically. While much of this trend may be due to higher incomes coupled with a desire for increased leisure, it appears that the retirement incentives of private pensions may also be inducing widespread retirement. For older workers covered by private pensions, pension accrual is typically substantial prior to specific ages and then becomes significantly negative after these ages. Such accrual profiles provide very substantial incentives to retire. Such incentives are the primary focus of this monograph.

Analysis of pension accrual can also provide insight into the structure of the labor market. Many economists view the labor market as primarily a spot market in which a worker is paid each year for work done that year; others view employers and workers as entering into long-term contractual arrangements which may be implicit as well as explicit. Under such arrangements, compensation for work done in the present may be paid in the future. Information on pension accrual can provide information on the empirical relevance of the contract versus spot market views of the labor market.

A third important reason for studying pension accrual concerns government policy towards "pension backloading." Pension backloading refers to pension plans that provide very little pension accrual up to a specific age and substantial pension accrual after a

1

specific age. This feature of pension plans typically means that pension benefits are much smaller for employees who change jobs than for those who don't, holding earnings constant. Much of the regulation of vesting rules contained in ERISA, the Employees Retirement Income Security Act of 1974, and in subsequent legislation reflects an effort to limit pension backloading. Despite these and related efforts, backloading remains a feature of a large fraction of defined benefit pension plans. The backloading under current plans is due to quite typical age-related and service-related provisions of normal and early retirement benefit formulae.

Other reasons for studying pension accrual include worker mobility, sex and age discrimination, firm valuation, and proper disclosure to workers of pension benefit information. Clearly, if the labor market is best characterized as a long-term contractual arrangement between workers and firms, then the future path of pension accrual is an important element of that contract. If future pension accrual is substantial, workers may be effectively "locked in" to their present firm. Thus, workers approaching the age of full vesting or of substantial pension accrual may delay switching jobs until they have exhausted pension accrual on their current jobs. Others may change jobs without fully appreciating the loss in potential pension accrual that such change entails.

Since defined benefit pension formulae are sex blind and since women typically live longer than men, the pension cost of employing women may exceed that for men in many firms. If firms are unable to pay women a smaller nonpension compensation, the total labor cost of hiring women will exceed that of hiring men and may mitigate against employment of women. Pension accrual also differs due to the age of the worker. If newly hired older workers accrue pension benefits at a faster rate than newly hired younger workers, and if firms cannot pay older workers less than younger workers, then firms may be less willing to hire older workers. Knowledge of vested pension accrual is of obvious importance to the proper valuation of firms since accrued vested benefits are a financial liability. While the accountants and actuaries of major U.S. corporations and unincorporated businesses calculate aggregate accrued vested liabilities, the accounting procedures vary widely. In addition, knowledge of a firm's overall liability is different from knowledge of the pension accrual of its particular workers. The complexity of pension benefit formulae calls into question whether employers and personnel managers fully understand the nature of pension compensation. The complexity also suggests that workers may not understand the extent of pension accrual. If workers are overvaluing their pension benefits, they may be accepting too little in the form of nonpension compensation. Alternatively, they may undervalue their pension benefits and seek too much in nonpension compensation. The complexity of pension accrual suggests the need for annual statements indicating each worker's accrued benefit and providing projections about future accrual.

This monograph examines pension accruals, both their size and their incentive effects, particularly with respect to retirement behavior. It combines (in parts of chapters 2, 3 and 4 and appendices I and II) the results of our previous research (Kotlikoff and Wise 1985 and 1987) on pension accrual in U.S. firms, with new findings (reported in chapters 5 and 6 and appendix III) on pension accrual and retirement behavior in one very large U.S. firm. The analysis relies primarily on two sources of data. The first is the Bureau of Labor Statistics' 1979 Level of Benefits Survey (BLS-LOB). This survey of 1469 establishments with 3,386,121 pension participants, provides extremely detailed information concerning pension benefits, vesting, and early retirement formulae, all of which are crucial inputs to the calculation of pension accruals. The second data set, denoted here as FIRM, contains the complete work histories of over 122,000 employees who were working at some time during the period 1981–1984 for a large Fortune 500 company. While the name of this company cannot be revealed, the company is in the service industry.

The BLS-LOB data are useful for exhibiting typical patterns of pension accrual as well as indicating variations across pension plans in accrual patterns. The FIRM data can be used to study the retirement response to age-pension-accrual profiles.

The monograph is organized as follows. The remainder of this introduction discusses more fully three key issues motivating the analysis of pension accrual. The first is the trend toward early retirement; the second is the question of pension backloading; and the third is the spot versus contract views of the labor market. Chapter 2 explains pension benefit accrual and illustrates age-pension-accrual profiles arising under typical pension plan provisions. The third chapter first describes the BLS-LOB data. Next it uses the Retirement History Survey (RHS) and the Current Population Survey (CPS) to calculate representative age-earnings profiles by age, sex, occupation, and industry. These age-earnings profiles are then used to study typical as well as unusual age-pension-accrual profiles among the universe of U.S. defined benefit plans. Chapter 4 uses the same data and procedures as chapter 3, but focuses on the pension costs of job mobility and differences by age, sex, industry and occupation in pension accrual. Chapter 5 begins with a presentation of the FIRM's data. Next it describes the FIRM's benefit formula in close detail. From the FIRM's accrual profile it is clear that most of the FIRM's employees have a very strong incentive to retire at the FIRM's early retirement age, age 55. Chapter 6 examines the retirement response to the FIRM's accrual profile. The final chapter summarizes the main findings of this study.

The principal conclusions of this monograph are:

(1) The age-accrual profiles of typical pension plans exhibit sharp discontinuities at the ages of vesting, early retirement and normal retirement.

(2) In most firms with defined benefit plans, pension accrual gives workers a very substantial incentive to leave the firm after the age of early retirement and an even greater incentive to leave after normal retirement age.

(3) The old age work disincentives of private pension plans typically are very large and exceed social security old age work disincentives.

(4) Government vesting and related legislation notwithstanding, sizeable pension backloading remains an important feature of a significant fraction of defined benefit plans.

(5) There is a very wide variation across pension plans in pension accrual profiles and, consequently, in retirement incentives.

(6) For younger workers in some firms the expected loss in pension benefits due to job change is quite substantial.

(7) For middle age and older male and female workers earning the same nonpension wage, there is a roughly 10 percent male-female difference in pension benefit accrual assuming average male and female mortality probabilities.

(8) Analysis of the retirement behavior in the FIRM indicates a very significant retirement response to the pattern of pension accrual.

(9) Over 50 percent of 50-year-old employees of the FIRM leave before age 60, and 90 percent leave before age 65. The jumps in departure rates at specific ages coincide precisely with the discontinuities (kink points) in pension and social security accrual.

(10) The FIRM's pension accrual increases the probability of workers age 55 leaving the FIRM before age 60 by approximately 30 percent, from 14 percent to 44 percent.

(11) The pattern of pension accrual with age is strongly at odds with a spot market view of the labor market.

The Trend Toward Early Retirement

The trend toward early retirement dates from the beginning of this century (Ransom and Sutch 1986). In 1900, the labor force participation rate of males 65 and older was 58.4 percent. By 1930, this rate had declined to 53.9 percent. The decline over the next 30 years, beginning essentially at the inception of social security, was substantial; the 1960 participation rate of older men was 33.1 percent. But an even bigger percentage decline has occurred since 1960; the most recent statistics record a 1986 labor force participation rate of older men of only 17.5 percent.

The trend toward early retirement has occurred despite an increase in life expectancy. The expected length of life for 20-year-olds at the turn of the century was roughly 45 years; the current figure is 50. At 65, life expectancy is now 16.8 years; at the turn of the century it was only 11.9 years. The trend toward early retirement has also occurred despite major increases in wage compensation; on average, annual real wage payments to workers have risen almost fourfold since 1900. A common explanation for the retirement trend is the increased demand for leisure associated with higher incomes. Like average annual real wage payments, real per capita income has increased enormously since 1900. The current figure measured in constant dollars is over four times the corresponding figure for 1900.

The acceleration in the rate of early retirement since 1960 appears to be due to factors other than increases in real income levels of the elderly, however. Many researchers have pointed to increases in social security benefits as a possible explanation (e.g., Hurd and Boskin 1984; Hausman and Wise 1985; Burtless 1986). Boskin (1977) stressed that social security's earnings test, which taxes back the social security benefits of workers whose earnings exceed rather small "exempt" amounts, may be an important cause of reduction in the labor force participation of older workers. Kotlikoff (1978) showed that many social security recipients adjust their labor supply to earn just under social security's exempt amounts.

Other researchers, particularly Blinder, Gordon, and Wise (1981), have cast doubt on the notion that social security induces early retirement, at least prior to age 65. They pointed out that between ages 62 (social security's early retirement age) and 65 (social security's normal retirement age) workers do not lose any social security benefits in present expected value if they continue to work, because by foregoing benefits between 62 and 65, the age 65 benefit is actuarially increased. These researchers also pointed out that there are recomputation features of social security's benefit calculation that constitute implicit subsidies to labor supply prior to age 65. After age 65, however, social security benefits are typically not increased enough if retirement is postponed to compensate for the reduced number of years that they will be received.

One may question whether social security beneficiaries are aware of and correctly understand provisions such as actuarial increases and benefit recomputations. In addition, it may well be that many social security beneficiaries are liquidity-constrained, in which case they may well need to start collecting social security benefits prior to age 65, and, once they become social security recipients they fall under the earnings test. Hurd and Boskin (1984) stress liquidity constraints and social security's income effects as important factors in inducing early retirement. They use the Retirement History Survey (RHS) data and report that "any way the data were analyzed we found a positive association between retirement probabilities and social security wealth." They conclude that most of the substantial decline in labor force participation of the young elderly that occurred between 1968 and 1973 can be traced to increases in social security benefits.

Blinder and Gordon (1980) and Burtless (1986) base their analyses of retirement behavior on the same data as Hurd and Boskin, but their conclusions about social security's impact on retirement differ. Blinder and Gordon find that "pension plans . . . provide powerful incentives to retire at the age of eligibility for the pension . . . (but) Social Security has a much weaker effect, if any, on retirement decisions." Burtless states that "Social Security is found to have a precisely measured, but small overall effect on retirement." According to Burtless "rising Social Security benefits in the 1970s played only a small role in the decline in the average male retirement age." Hausman and Wise (1984) reach a similar conclusion in their analysis of the RHS data. They report that social security has an important effect on retirement, but that social security benefit increases in the early 1970s provide only a partial explanation for the reduced labor force participation over that period.

The study of Burtless and Moffitt (1984) is also based on the RHS, but it differs from Burtless (1986) in that it considers both retirement age and postretirement choice of hours of work. The conclusion from this analysis is also that social security has a statistically significant, but small effect on the age of retirement and that its effects operate through the level of social security benefits and the age at which benefits become available, rather than through social security's earnings test. Other analyses by Burkhauser and Quinn (1983); Fields and Mitchell (1984a, b); and Diamond and Hausman (1984) also report small social security effects.

Gustman and Steinmeier's (1983, 1985, 1986a, 1986b) analyses of retirement include the possibility of partial retirement at a reduced wage. Their studies, also based on the Retirement History Survey, suggest an important role of both social security and pensions in retirement decisions; indeed in their (1983) paper they report that ". . . the combined effects of Social Security and pension benefits and mandatory retirement is to cause the percentage of individuals working full-time at age 66 to fall by 18.9 percentage points."

While increases in social security benefits and the work disincentive from social security's earnings test may help explain reductions in labor force participation after age 62, these factors cannot explain increased retirement between ages 55 and 61. Since 1960, the labor force participation rate of males in this age range has declined significantly. As demonstrated in this monograph, private pensions appear to be playing an important role in inducing retirement at these ages as well as at age 62 and beyond; the work disincentives at specific ages arising under many defined benefit pension plans are quite substantial; indeed, they are often larger than those arising from social security (even ignoring issues of actuarial increases and benefit recomputation).

Indeed the effect on retirement that has been attributed to social security may largely reflect a failure to control for private pension plan provisions. Like social security, most private pension plans provide a very large penalty for working after 65; but none of the studies summarized above were able to control for the precise provisions of private plans.

Despite the potential importance of private pensions in inducing early retirement, there have been very few studies relating retirement to pension incentives. The reason is simply the limited available data detailing employee work histories together with the specific details of the employer's pension plan. There is an excellent Department of Labor data set detailing both work histories and pension plan provision for a representative sample of U.S. pension plans, but these data have not been made available to the public because of confidentiality concerns. Some limited analysis for the Department of Labor of these data by Gary Fields and Olivia Mitchell (1984a) indicates a significant retirement response to pension incentives.

Pension Backloading

Prior to ERISA, companies often required as many as 25 years of service for pension vesting. To protect workers from being dismissed, falling ill, or leaving their employment for other reasons immediately prior to becoming vested, ERISA mandated 100 percent vesting within 10 years of initial participation in a pension plan. The 10-year vesting rule was reduced to 5 years in the 1986 Tax Reform Act.

The intent of the vesting provisions of ERISA and the 1986 Tax Reform Act was surely to limit the extent of backloading of vested pension accrual. While it is true that delaying vesting is a mechanism for delaying the vested accrual of pension benefits, it is only one such mechanism. As this monograph makes clear, there are numerous other pension plan provisions determining the age pattern of vested accrual. These include numerous basic benefit formulae, provisions formulae determining supplemental benefits, rates of early retirement benefit reduction, and social security offset provisions. For a significant proportion of defined benefit pension plans, these and related features lead to very substantial backloading of accrued vested pension benefits. The FIRM's pension plan discussed in chapter 5 is a case in point. In this plan there is modest accrual of vested benefits prior to the plan's early retirement age and substantial pension accrual at the early retirement age. As a consequence, a worker who leaves the FIRM just prior to its early retirement age will receive a rather limited pension when compared to the pension of a worker who stays through the age of early retirement. The impact of these provisions is thus quite similar to those that would arise under a very long service requirement for vesting.

We are not suggesting that employers are deliberately designing defined benefit plans to circumvent the will of Congress; indeed, employers as well as workers may be unaware of the extent of backloading of pension accrual. (In the case of our FIRM, the extent of backloading was a surprise to several of the plan administrators.) What we are suggesting is that such backloading of vested pension accrual appears contrary to the intent of the vesting legislation and merits careful study by Congress.

Spot Versus Contract Theories of the Labor Market and the Use of Pension Accruals to Test these Theories

Under the spot market view of the labor market, the sum of annual nonpension compensation and annual pension accrual should equal the worker's annual output. If the worker's annual output is, for example, constant independent of age, any increases (decreases) with age in pension accrual should be offset dollar for dollar by decreases (increases) at the corresponding ages in nonpension compensation. While only one worker's output may change with age, it is unlikely to change precipitously from one age to another. In contrast, pension accrual can change dramatically with age, requiring offsetting dramatic changes in nonpension compensation according to the spot market view.

Understanding the extent of contractual arrangements between workers and firms is important for a host of economic issues ranging from the degree of wage flexibility over the business cycle to the availability of human capital insurance within the firm. Discriminating between "spot" and "long-term contract" views of the labor market is also critical for evaluating numerous questions specific to private pensions. One such question is whether workers and employers fully appreciate how complex pension plan provisions alter a firm's total compensation package. Evidence that labor markets closely accord with the predictions of a spot market would suggest rather small information problems. Equally productive workers, in this case, receive identical total annual remuneration regardless of their current employer or the specifics of the employer's pension plan.

A second question involves proper disclosure and valuation of a pension plan's net financial liabilities. In a spot market setting, an employer's net liability corresponds simply to the accrued value of vested pension benefits. Additional pension liabilities projected to arise from future employment, in such a setting, are matched dollar for dollar by future projected revenues associated with the worker's continued employment. The excess of projected over accrued liabilities should not, therefore, affect a firm's valuation and suggests no case for estimating and disclosing projected pension liabilities. Under a long-term contract arrangement, on the other hand, revenue from continued employment need not match the accrual of future pension liabilities, plus the payment of wages, and the disclosure of projected rather than accrued liabilities is potentially more relevant for firm financial valuation.

A third question is the effect of pensions on labor mobility and hiring practices. In a spot market environment, the particular and quite peculiar rates of pension benefit accrual with age described in this monograph would have no consequences for labor mobility, since offsetting increases or reductions in direct wage compensation would leave the worker indifferent between staying on the current job or switching to another job offering an identical amount of total compensation. A spot market would also entail flexibility in wage compensation sufficient to permit hiring equally productive old and young, black and white, male and female workers, despite differences in their accrual of vested pension benefits reflecting age, race, and sex-specific mortality probabilities. Long-term contractual agreements, in contrast, may leave less flexibility to accommodate differences in individual circumstances.

Given knowledge of a worker's current and previous level of earnings, and the benefit and retirement provisions of his pension plan, one could, in principle, directly test the spot market hypothesis by checking whether, in each year, the sum of the increment to a worker's accrued vested pension benefits plus his wage compensation equalled his marginal product.[1] Unfortunately, a worker's marginal product is unobservable and difficult to estimate. This data limitation restricts, but, by no means precludes, inferences about spot versus contractual labor market arrangements.

As stated, the sum of the assumed age-earnings profile, measured in constant dollars, and the associated real pension accrual profile equals, under the spot market assumption, the age-marginal productivity profile. Hypothetical age-marginal productivity profiles derived in this manner exhibit quite sharp or implausible discontinuities at two critical ages, the age of full vesting, for plans with cliff vesting, and the early retirement age, for plans permitting early retirement on better than actuarially fair terms.[2] Making reasonable assumptions concerning age-earnings profiles and interest rates, we find sizeable discontinuities (often as large as 40 percent) in hypothetical age-marginal productivity profiles for a large fraction of firms with defined benefit plans. An alternative statement of these findings is that for smoothly shaped age-marginal product schedules, wage compensation must potentially fall or rise by roughly 40 percent of the wage at critical ages to satisfy conditions of spot market equilibrium. These figures appear sufficiently large to rule out the hypothesis of annual spot clearing for a large segment of the U.S. labor market.

As Lazear's (1983) insightful study points out, the present expected value of accrued pension benefits represents a form of severance pay for workers who choose to separate from the firm. Such severance pay would naturally arise in contractual settings in which workers are paid (in wages) less than their marginal products. As the worker ages, the average value of this "severance pay" rises until the age of normal retirement, according to our findings. In a contractual setting, the implication of our finding of positive average pension accrual at all ages prior to normal retirement is that average real wages represent a lower bound for the average marginal product of workers covered by our sample of plans, up to the age of normal retirement. But after that age, accrual is typically negative, suggesting that the wage exceeds marginal product at some age. It is important to emphasize, however, that we find large deviations from the average, with large negative accruals after the age of early retirement in many plans. And for other plans with positive pension accruals between early and normal retirement, the decline in pension accrual from a large positive number to a small positive number in this age interval is, itself, a significant retirement incentive.

Finally, an additional implication of these findings is that compensating differential studies of the tradeoff between wages and pension benefits, if they are to be meaningful, cannot be based on cross-section evidence at a point in time. To understand the relationship between compensation in the form of wages versus pension benefits, one must consider the receipt of both over a long period of employment.

2
Understanding Pension Benefit Accrual

Defining Pension Accrual

Consider a worker who is paid in two forms: salary and pension compensation. Pension compensation for working a year is the increase in pension wealth during that year and is called pension accrual. It is the difference between the present expected value of vested future benefits at the beginning and the end of the year. More formally, vested pension benefit accrual at age a, I(a), equals the difference between pension wealth at age a + 1, Pw(a+1), and pension wealth at age a, Pw(a), accumulated to age a + 1 at the nominal interest rate r, i.e.:

$$(1) \quad I(a) = Pw(a+1) - Pw(a)(1+r).$$

Pension wealth at age a is defined as the expected value of vested pension benefits discounted to age a. Intuitively, Pw(a) can be thought of as the worker's pension bank account. If I(a) equals zero, the worker continuing employment with the firm at age a has exactly the same pension wealth at age a+1 as an identically situated worker who terminates employment at age a. Pension accrual is thus the increment to pension wealth in excess of the return on the previously accumulated pension bank account.

The shape of pension accrual profiles, analogous to age-earnings profiles, can be understood by considering a stylized pension plan. The normal retirement age assumed for this stylized plan is 65. Assume, for the moment, that the plan has no early retirement option and that 100 percent vesting occurs in the 10th year of service. The retirement benefit of the stylized plan equals a constant λ multiplied by the product of final year's earnings and service. There is no effect of receipt of social security benefits. Let B(a,t) denote the pension benefit available at the plan's normal retirement age to the worker

13

who terminates employment with the plan sponsor at age a after t years of service. The relationship between B(a,t) and the worker's wage at age a, W(a), is simply:

(2) $B(a,t) = \lambda W(a)t$.

If the worker continues to work for another year, the benefit at the end of the year is:

(3) $B(a+1,t+1) = \lambda W(a+1)(t+1)$.

The difference in benefits between age a and age a+1, $\lambda[W(a+1)(t+1) - W(a)t]$, is depicted by the difference in the areas of the large rectangles in figure 2.1, except for the constant λ. The greater the wage increase, the greater the increase in pension benefits. Benefits would decrease if the wage declined enough.[3] Pension accrual is not simply the change in the benefit, however; rather it is

FIGURE 2.1 – Pension accrual between ages a and a+1

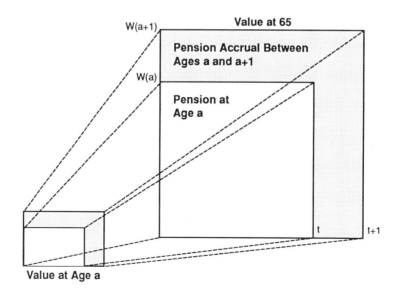

the change in the present value of expected future benefits. The present value of benefits at age a is given by:

$$(4) \quad Pw(a) = B(a,t)A(65)(1+r)^{-(65-a)}$$
$$= \lambda W(a)tA(65)(1+r)^{-(65-a)}.$$

The term $A(65)$ indicates the value at age 65 of a dollar of pension benefits received from age 65 until death. It represents an actuarial calculation that accounts for the likelihood that a person will be living at each age in the future after age 65 and discounts the benefits at the rate of interest, r. The term $(1+r)^{-(65-a)}$ transforms the stock of pension wealth at age 65 to its present value, at age a. To keep the formula simple, we assume a zero probability of death prior to age 65. The present value of pension wealth at age $a+1$ is

$$(5) \quad Pw(a+1) = B(a+1,t+1)A(65)(1+r)^{-(65-a-1)}$$
$$= \lambda W(a+1)(t+1)A(65)(1+r)^{-(65-a-1)}.$$

The increment to pension wealth between a and $a+1$, pension accrual, is given by

$$(6) \quad I(a) = Pw(a+1) - Pw(a)(1+r)$$
$$= [(1+r)^{-(65-a-1)}] \; [W(a+1)(t+1) - W(a)t]\lambda A(65).$$

The term in the second set of brackets is simply the change in the pension benefit at 65 due to working an additional year; it is represented by the difference in the large rectangles in figure 2.1. Multiplying this term by $\lambda A(65)$, it gives the change in the value of pension wealth at age 65. The term in the first set of brackets is the discount factor that transforms the change to its present value, at age a. The present value of the change is represented by the difference in the small rectangles in figure 2.1. Notice that the accrual will be very small if age a is much less than 65, say 30. The present value declines exponentially with the difference between a and 65. At age 64 the discount factor is 1, at 63 it is $1/(1+r)$, at 62 it is $1/(1+r)^2$, etc. In other words, as the age at which benefits are available draws nearer, the accrual grows exponentially because of the discounting. In addition, pension accrual will be greater the greater the increase in wages. In the graphs that follow, pension accrual at age a is shown as a percent of the wage at that age. This ratio is denoted by R(a,t) and is defined by:

(7) $R(a,t) = I(a)/W(a)$.

Under the provisions of this stylized plan, accrual as a proportion of the wage is shown by the line in figure 2.2 labeled "Retirement at 65 Only," indicating that the plan has no early retirement option. The nominal wage growth incorporated in the age-earnings profile assumes moderate life cycle growth in real wages plus a 6 percent rate of inflation. A 3 percent real interest rate (9 percent nominal rate) is also assumed.[4] Accrual is zero before vesting. In the example, vesting occurs after 10 years of service, at age 40. This cliff

FIGURE 2.2 – Pension increments as a percentage of salary, by age, for plans with an early retirement option versus retirement at 65. (6% wage inflation rate)

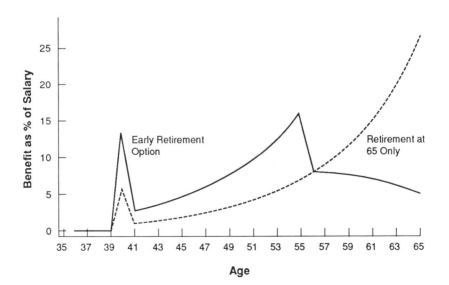

vesting produces a spike in the accrual profile at this age. At age 41, the accrual is smaller because it equals only the difference in pension wealth at ages 40 and 41, whereas the accrual at 40 is total pension wealth accrued in the first 10 years of service (since accrued vested pension wealth at age 39 is zero). In subsequent years, accrual grows exponentially as age approaches 65, as long as wage growth is sufficiently large, as described above. These provisions create an incentive to stay with the firm until age 65, since pension accrual is increasing. This attribute of the standard defined benefit plan is called backloading.

Unlike the plan described thus far, most defined benefit plans have early retirement provisions. Such provisions typically have a dramatic effect on the pension accrual profile. The accrual under the stylized plan, but with an actuarially unfair early retirement option at age 55, is shown in the profile labeled "Early Retirement Option" in figure 2.2. Figure 2.3 repeats figure 2.2 but under the as-

FIGURE 2.3 – Pension increments as a percentage of salary, by age, for plans with an early retirement option versus retirement at 65. (0% wage inflation,, 10% real interest rate)

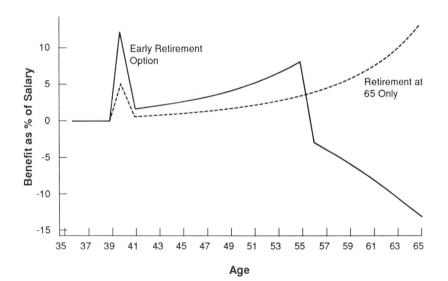

sumptions of a 10 percent interest rate and no growth in wages by age. For the profile with the early retirement option, accrual rates after age 55 are substantially negative, approaching −15 percent of salary at age 65. With no early retirement option, on the other hand, accrual rates are always positive. We now discuss without the use of explicit formulae why the early retirement option can alter the shape of age-pension-accrual profiles. The formulae are presented in appendix I.

The important feature of the typical early retirement option is that the early retirement benefit reduction is less than actuarially fair. That is, benefits are not reduced enough to offset the fact that they will be received for more years. The present value of pension wealth, if receipt of benefits begins at 55, is larger than if receipt begins at any later age. Thus at any age younger than 55, the pension wealth that the worker is entitled to, were he to leave the firm at age a, is the present value of benefits if their receipt begins at 55. The calculation that gives the present value at age a of benefits available at age 55, instead of at 65, yields an accrual profile that increases exponentially to age 55, instead of 65. Were the early retirement reduction actuarially fair, the profile would look just like the one with no early retirement. The present value of pension wealth would be independent of the age between 55 and 65 that benefits were first received. Thus the "retirement at 65 only" profile could also be labeled "actuarially fair accrual rates," since, by definition, an actuarially fair early retirement reduction formula produces an accrual profile that is independent of the age at which benefits are first received.

With early retirement with less than actuarial reduction, accrual declines after age 55. The are three reasons for this: (1) Prior to age 55 an increment in pension benefits has a higher present value as the age, 55, at which they can be received draws nearer. After 55, benefits are available immediately. Unlike benefits prior to age 55, benefits at 56, for example, are *not* discounted relative to those at 57 because the worker doesn't have to wait a year longer to receive them. This reduces accrual compared to the accrual just before age 55. (2) Before age 55 the present value of benefits at age a and at age $a+1$, conditional on reaching the age of early retirement, are both based on the receipt of benefits from age 55 until death. After 55, however, if retirement is postponed the number of years that benefits will be received declines, tending to lower their present value. (3) After early retirement, the smaller the reduction factor the closer pension wealth at age a will be to wealth at age $a+1$, reducing the accrual between a and $a+1$. The lower the reduction factor, the lower the accrual. The reduction factors for many plans are quite small. If there were no reduction, the benefit at age a would be the same as at age $a+1$, and the present value of benefits starting at a I 1 would tend to be lower than at age a because they would be received for one year less. Accrual before the early retirement age is not affected by the early retirement reduction factor. Before the early retirement age, the *higher* the discount rate r, the greater the *increase* in the accrual rate as age approaches 55. After 55, the *lower* the early retirement reduction factor, the greater the decline in accrual with age. In summary, remaining with the firm after the early retirement age means foregoing the option of accepting benefits on advantageous terms. In addition to the three factors just mentioned, the pension accrual is of course affected by the increase (or decrease) in the wage.

As subsequent exposition will show, at least until the 1986 Age Discrimination Act, accrual typically declined sharply at age 65, and was usually negative thereafter, whether or not the plan had an early retirement option. The Age Discrimination Act, which postdates the plans described in this monograph, requires the continued crediting of service for workers beyond the age of normal retirement. This law lessens, somewhat, the sharp drop in pension accrual after normal retirement.

While the preceding description is suggestive of the general shape of accrual rate profiles, there are few earnings-based plans with features as simple as the early retirement option plan considered here. In addition to more complicated rules for plan participation and vesting that often involve age as well as service requirements, there are a variety of methods of computing earnings bases, including career averages, and averages of earnings, possibly highest earnings, over a specified period or number of years. Reduction rates for early retirement are often a specified function of age as well as length of service. Some plans allow no further accrual after a given number of years of service.

Roughly 30 percent of defined benefit participants belong to plans that are integrated with social security. There are two, not necessarily independent, important forms of "integration." One involves a "step rate" benefit formula that uses a different value for the percentage of the product of earnings times service for levels of earnings below and levels above specified values. The second is referred to as an "offset" formula which reduces pension benefits by some fraction of the participant's basic social security benefit. Many of the offset plans set ceilings on the extent of the offset. A minority of plans, in particular, those with social security offset formulae, provide supplemental benefits for early retirees prior to their receipt of social security benefits.

The supplemental benefit formulae can also be quite involved, incorporating both the participant's age and service in the calculation. There are also plans that use one benefit formula to compute early retirement benefits and a different formula to determine normal retirement benefits. In addition to these earnings-related plans, a significant number of plans covering over 40 percent of defined benefit participants calculate benefits independent of the participant's earnings history (Kotlikoff and Smith 1983, table 4.5.1). These formulae can also be quite complex. There are other plans that are earnings-related, but provide differing flat benefit amounts based on the participant's earnings level. Finally, there are plans that specify minimum and maximum benefit levels. Each of these additional features can significantly alter the profile of accrual rates by age, especially the extent of discontinuities in the profile. Our analysis of pension plans in this monograph takes account of a great number of those complexities.

The assumption of constant nominal interest rates implies a quite different pattern of pension accrual than would occur with variable interest rates. Changes in long term nominal interest rates produce capital gains and losses on previously accumulated pension wealth that do not directly affect pension accrual. A time path of varying interest rates around a constant mean would produce a much more discontinuous age-pension accrual profile than those in figures 2.1 and 2.2 and in other diagrams in this monograph.

Additional Features of Accrual Profiles and Sensitivity to Wage Inflation and Interest Rates

The Interest Rate

Figure 2.4 depicts three accrual rate profiles for a worker who begins participating at age 30 in a defined benefit plan like that described above. The plan calculates normal retirement benefits as 1 percent of average earnings over the last five years of service times years of service. Benefits are reduced by 3 percent for each year that early retirement precedes normal retirement. Cliff vesting occurs after 10 years. The early and normal retirement ages are 55 and 65

FIGURE 2.4 – Pension increments as a percentage of salary, by age, for a wage stream with 6% inflation discounted at real interest rates of 3%, 6% and 9%.

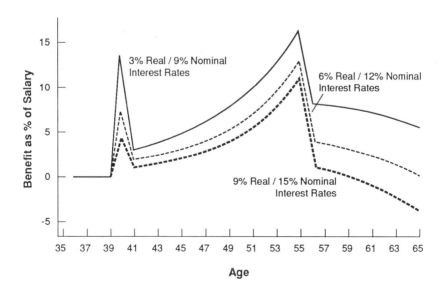

respectively. Nominal wage growth is determined by two factors, a cross-sectional profile of "merit" increases by age and an assumed economywide rate of wage inflation. The merit profile involves approximately a 50 percent growth in real wages between ages 30 and 50 and very little growth from 50 to 65. The rate of wage inflation incorporates both across-the-board increases in labor productivity and the price level.

As in the comparison of figures 2.2 and 2.3 above, figure 2.4 shows the sensitivity of the profiles to the real interest rate, the rate at which future benefits are discounted. The top profile incorporates a 6 percent rate of inflation and a 9 percent nominal (3 percent real) interest rate. The bottom profile incorporates 6 percent nominal wage growth, but a 15 percent nominal interest rate. The intermediate profile in figure 2.4 is based on 6 percent wage growth and a 12 percent nominal interest rate. It yields increments at 65 that are approximately zero. These figures demonstrate that, ceteris paribus, higher nominal interest rates, whether due to higher real rates or higher inflation premia, produce lower rates of pension accrual. While real interest rates as high as 10 percent are well above historic after-tax real returns, they seem plausible as risk adjusted rates that would be used by potentially liquidity-constrained workers. The figures also indicate that under these plan provisions a considerable gap between nominal interest rates and wage growth rates is needed to produce negative accrual rates before age 65.

Inflation

The three profiles in figure 2.5 differ both in their assumed rates of wage inflation and nominal interest, but incorporate the same 3 percent real interest rate. The 2 percent wage inflation profile discounts pension benefits at a 5 percent nominal rate, while the 6 and 10 percent wage inflation profiles are based on 9 and 13 percent nominal interest rates, respectively.

The major effect of the assumptions about wage growth and nominal interest rates is on the "vesting spike." These assumptions produce vesting spikes ranging from 5 to 37 percent of wages at age 40. The intermediate wage and interest rate assumption produces a 14 percent spike at cliff vesting.

FIGURE 2.5 – Pension increments as a percentage of salary, by age, for wage inflation of 2%, 6% and 10%. Benefits discounted at a 3% real interest rate.

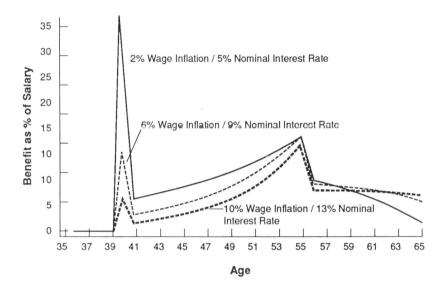

Age of Joining the Plan

Accrual rate profiles for workers joining the pension plan at ages 30, 40, and 50 are presented in figure 2.6, based on the intermediate wage and interest rate assumptions of figure 2.4. The vesting spikes for the three profiles are 14, 36, and 66 percent of the corresponding wage at ages 40, 50, and 60. While vesting at these latter ages is much less common than prior to age 40, Kotlikoff and Smith (1983, table 3.6.5) report that over a quarter of current defined benefit pension recipients retired with 20 or fewer years of service.

Job Change

Figure 2.6 is constructed under the assumption that the workers of the same age receive identical wage compensation. Thus the diagram also indicates the potential loss in accrued pension benefits for workers who switch jobs, but receive the same wage compensation in the new job and are covered by the same pension plan.

FIGURE 2.6 – Pension increments as a percentage of salary, by age, for an employee beginning work at 31, 41 and 51. (6% wage inflation, 3% real interest rate)

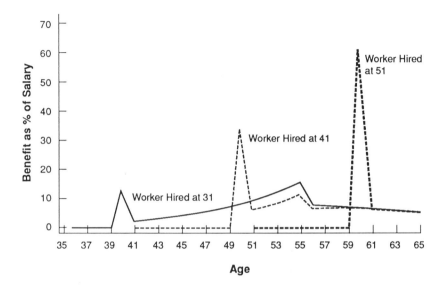

Figure 2.7 illustrates the cost of job change with no early retirement option. It should be compared with figure 2.6. The loss is substantially greater without the early retirement option. The plans represented in the two diagrams are the same except that in figure 2.7 the early retirement reduction schedule is assumed to be actuarially fair (equivalently, there is no early retirement option). Again, the top line of this graph shows the accrual rate under our plan for a person who starts work at age 30 (with 6 percent wage inflation and a 3 percent real interest rate). A person with one job change would accumulate benefits up to age 41 according to the top curve, but then would accumulate benefits according to the curve labelled "age 41." Note that no benefits would be accumulated for the first 10 years. The difference in accumulated pension benefits at age 65 reflects the difference in the areas under the two accrual paths. This difference could be very substantial and depends, of course, both on when job changes occur and how frequently they occur.

FIGURE 2.7 – Pension increments as a percentage of salary, by age, for an employee beginning work at 31, 41 and 51, with no early retirement option. (6% wage inflation, 3% real interest rate)

It is also important to note that the loss in accrued benefits from job change in this example is not due solely to vesting; in figure 2.7, accrual in years after vesting occurs is larger for a worker remaining on the same job for 35 years than for a worker who changes jobs (literally pension plans). This lower accrual beyond vesting for later plan entrants results from the interaction of service and wage growth in earnings-based defined benefit pension formulae. To see the nature of this interaction, consider a plan with immediate vesting that pays 2 percent of final year's salary times years of service. For a worker experiencing positive wage growth who is employed for, say, 30 years and retires at 60, the pension benefit is 2 percent of the age 60 salary times 30. If this same worker experiencing the same wage growth were to change jobs each year, joining an identical plan, his benefit would equal 2 percent times the sum of the 30 annual salaries. Assuming positive wage growth, the pension benefit of the former worker which is based on the age 60 salary will exceed that of the latter worker whose benefit is primarily based on the lower earnings received in earlier years of his career. In effect, defined benefit plans that base benefits on end-of-career earnings, index benefits to the wage.

Summary

Pension accrual refers to the annual compensation paid to a worker through a firm's pension plan. Pension accrual is defined as the addition to the worker's pension wealth that is above and beyond interest earned on previously accumulated pension wealth. Various defined benefit pension provisions, including basic and supplemental benefit formulae, ages of early and normal retirement, and early retirement reduction factors, are important factors influencing pension accrual.

The profile of pension accrual is particularly sensitive to early retirement provisions. Less than actuarial reduction of early retirement benefits or the provision of supplemental benefits to those who take early retirement can lead to accrual profiles that increase sharply at the age of early retirement. In such plans there is potentially a very large incentive to remain with the firm through the age of early retirement. After the age of early retirement and certainly after the age of normal retirement, pension accrual may be very small if not negative and may, therefore, induce workers to retire. This is the notion of the wage carrot and the pension stick. The wage provides a general incentive to remain with the firm, but the pension plan after a certain point in time may greatly penalize workers who fail to retire.

In addition to depending on the particular plan provisions, the shapes and levels of accrual profiles are quite sensitive to the assumed rates of interest, wage growth, and inflation. In the illustrations of this chapter, variations in these assumptions produced accrual spikes at vesting ranging from 5 percent to 37 percent of wages. The accrual profiles also depend on the age at which the worker begins participating in the pension plan. For workers who begin participating late in life, the pension spike at vesting can be as large as two-thirds of the wage.

Another way to make the point that defined benefit plans give workers incentives to remain with the plan sponsor, at least through early retirement, is to demonstrate the possible loss in pension benefits suffered by workers who change jobs. Again, depending on the plan's precise provisions, the choice of economic assumptions, and the pension on the job to which a worker moves, pensions may impose considerable costs to job mobility for workers of certain ages and with certain amounts of service. For other workers, such as those who are eligible for early retirement, the pension cost of job change may be negative, and pensions may induce more job mobility.

3
Pension Accrual in the BLS-LOB Data

In this chapter we examine accrual ratios for earnings-based and flat benefit (nonearnings-based) defined benefit plans from the BLS-LOB survey. The chapter begins with a brief description of the BLS-LOB data. The next section describes the creation of wage profiles used to form pension accrual profiles. Earnings-based plans are considered in the third section, while the final section examines flat benefit plans. Variation in pension accrual profiles due to differences in retirement ages is the topic of the third section, followed by a discussion of the wide variation among plans for given combinations of early and normal retirement ages. Next, the effect of social security offset provisions are considered, and then the effects of alternative postnormal-retirement provisions are examined. These analyses are followed by a consideration of the effects on accrual profiles of early and normal retirement supplements.

The BLS-LOB Data

The BLS-LOB (1979) establishments constitute a subsample of the 1979 National Survey of Professional, Administrative, Technical and Clerical Pay. Based on the file's population weights, this subsample covers 17,965,282 private pension plan participants in the U.S., which is slightly over half of all 1979 private pension participants. The subsample's universe consists of all firms with over 100 employees with the exception of mining, construction and retail trade establishments where the minimum firm size was 250 employees and service establishments where the minimum firm size was 50 employees. The BLS-LOB survey contains 3,248 plans, of which the BLS labeled 2,492 as "usable." Our master sample consists of 2,343 of these 2,492 plans. This study focuses on 1,183 plans that determine benefits based on past earnings and that specify cliff vesting at 10 years of service.

Sampled establishments were requested to report work schedules and information about 11 different types of fringe benefits. This information was provided for each of three occupational groups: managers, sales workers, and office workers. The BLS-LOB (1979) pension benefits tape consists of establishment records for each occupational group that detail features of pension benefit plans covering the particular occupational group in question. Unfortunately, firm identifiers are intentionally excluded from the computer record; hence, it is impossible to reconstruct the actual pension characteristics of the initial establishment. The data can, however, be used to estimate industrywide or occupationwide values of pension variables.

The BLS-LOB data provide great detail concerning pension plan provisions. In computing the pension-accrued profiles discussed in this and the following chapter, we went to considerable pains to program each of the key pension provisions influencing pension accrual. In many cases this required writing numerous elaborate subroutines that were applicable to only a few of the pension plans.

Wage Profiles Used to Examine Pension Accrual in the BLS-LOB Plans

To calculate average pension benefit increments by industry-occupation group for a given length of employment we need estimates of age-wage profiles for each group. It is particularly important that assumptions about the wage profiles of older workers be as realistic as possible. It is clear from the discussion in chapter 2 that wage growth has an important effect on pension accrual. Wage growth affects compensation for future work directly, and indirectly, through its effect on pension accrual. Without lengthy longitudinal records on individuals, we have no completely satisfactory way of estimating age-wage profiles. The Retirement History Survey (RHS), however, does provide some longitudinal data for older workers.[5] We first discuss evidence from these data and then present estimated age-wage profiles based on the Current Population Survey (CPS) data. For older workers, the two sources of data provide roughly consistent evidence.

The age-wage profiles appropriate for determining pension accrual are clearly those pertaining to workers staying in the same firm, thus tenure as well as age should be included in the analysis of earnings by age. Our accrual profiles also assume full-time employment. Hence, wage rates per unit of time is the appropriate earnings concept for our purposes. While conventionally computed age-earnings profiles sometimes show a downward trend for older workers, this appears due, in part, to a reduction in hours worked and, in part, to the mix of full-time and part-time workers in the sample.

Evidence from the Retirement History Survey

The RHS data is based on a sample of persons who were first surveyed in 1969 when they were between 58 and 63. These respondents were resurveyed every two years until 1979. Table 3.1 shows the means of hourly wages by age and year for persons who reported an hourly wage rate and who were not partially or fully retired in a given year. For a given calendar year, these data in general show little decline in wage rates at least through age 63 or 64. The number of observations per cell is fairly small since the cells only include older individuals who are still working. Possibly those whose wage rates would have fallen from one year to the next are less likely to be in the sample. Analogous calculations showing the median of annual salaries of persons who reported weekly, monthly, or annual salaries, are presented in table 3.2. Here again, in the cross-section, there are relatively constant real salary levels through age 64 among persons who are not retired, although there seems to be some decline on average.

The accrual calculations require, however, nominal wage profiles. From both tables 3.1 and 3.2, it is clear that nominal wages of older workers increased rather rapidly over this period. A more precise indication of nominal increases is shown in table 3.3 for all persons who reported weekly, monthly, or annual salaries. The entry corresponding to age 58–60 and the year 1969–71 is the median salary increase between 1969 and 1971 for all persons who were 58 in 1969 and who reported salary figures in both 1969 and 1971. The other entries are calculated in an analogous manner. The table shows substantial nominal increases over this period, on the order of 6 percent per year on average. (The entries pertain to a two-year interval.)

Table 3.1
Means of Hourly Wages for Nonself-Employed Males,
by Age and Year

Age	Year						All Years
	1969	1971	1973	1975	1977	1979	
58	3.03						3.03
	(134)						(134)
59	3.36						3.36
	(159)						(159)
60	3.14	3.25					3.19
	(155)	(154)					(309)
61	3.05	3.36					3.21
	(130)	(149)					(279)
62	3.12	3.50	3.89				3.48
	(125)	(134)	(107)				(366)
63	2.91	3.30	4.10				3.44
	(93)	(115)	(103)				(311)
64		3.41	3.53	4.03			3.63
		(74)	(80)	(61)			(215)
65		3.44	3.15	3.54			3.39
		(44)	(34)	(41)			(119)
66			3.45	3.59	4.62		3.82
			(24)	(24)	(18)		(66)
67			3.24	2.83	3.48		3.24
			(21)	(13)	(22)		(56)
68				3.85	4.34	4.42	4.17
				(14)	(14)	(8)	(36)
69				3.60	2.71	3.82	3.30
				(6)	(9)	(7)	(22)
70					3.25	4.45	3.74
					(10)	(7)	(17)
71					4.25	4.16	4.21
					(7)	(4)	(11)
72						3.21	3.21
						(7)	(7)
73						4.42	4.42
						(2)	(2)

Source: *Retirement History Survey.* Excludes people who say they are partially or fully retired.
The number of observations used to calculate the associated value is recorded in parenthesis.

Table 3.2
Medians of Annual Salary for Nonself-Employed Males,
by Age and Year

Age	Year						All Years
	1969	1971	1973	1975	1977	1979	
58	7494 (666)						7494 (666)
59	7280 (733)						7280 (733)
60	7280 (683)	8372 (485)					7800 (1168)
61	7280 (690)	8100 (563)					7600 (1253)
62	7280 (591)	8216 (453)	9850 (322)				8008 (1366)
63	7225 (454)	8000 (413)	8800 (339)				7860 (1206)
64		8000 (403)	9100 (303)	10088 (246)			9000 (952)
65		7800 (179)	8200 (151)	9480 (146)			8320 (476)
66			8944 (110)	9200 (107)	11600 (76)		9663 (293)
67			8320 (91)	8942 (90)	11830 (56)		9048 (237)
68				9284 (70)	8541 (48)	6600 (18)	8998 (136)
69				8913 (54)	10089 (42)	4225 (8)	9360 (104)
70					7850 (30)	3750 (12)	6703 (42)
71					8525 (23)	4160 (10)	7380 (33)
72						3016 (13)	3016 (13)
73						7800 (9)	7800 (9)

Source: *Retirement History Survey*. Excludes people who say they are partially or fully retired. The number of observations used to calculate the associated value is recorded in parenthesis.

Table 3.3
**Median Percent Changes in Annual Salary for Nonself-Employed Males,
by Age and Year**

Age	Year					All Years
	1969–71	1971–73	1973–75	1975–77	1977–79	
58–60	13.0 (423)					13.0 (423)
59–61	12.5 (486)					12.5 (486)
60–62	12.5 (393)	12.6 (264)				12.5 (657)
61–63	11.7 (354)	11.0 (280)				11.1 (634)
62–64	11.3 (346)	11.7 (237)	13.3 (170)			11.5 (753)
63–65	10.4 (148)	11.1 (118)	11.1 (101)			11.1 (367)
64–66		12.9 (86)	12.1 (83)	10.5 (64)		12.2 (233)
65–67		9.5 (58)	12.5 (54)	11.4 (45)		10.8 (157)
66–68			10.8 (47)	12.8 (37)	12.9 (10)	11.8 (94)
67–69			6.4 (41)	10.1 (36)	6.2 (3)	8.3 (80)
68–70				10.6 (18)	29.8 (3)	13.3 (21)
69–71				12.5 (20)	17.5 (2)	12.5 (22)
70–72					13.1 (2)	13.1 (2)
71–73					15.4 (1)	15.4 (1)

Source: *Retirement History Survey*. Excluded people who say they are partially or fully retired. The number of observations used to calculate the associated value is recorded in parenthesis.

Considering the average increments by age in the last column, there is some evidence that the increases declined somewhat with age. At least through 1977—after which our sample sizes are very small—it appears that salary increases for these older workers were, in general, keeping up with price increases. The percent increases in the Consumer Price Index (CPI) for the years 1969 to 1977 were as follows:

Year	CPI
1969	6.1
1970	5.5
1971	3.4
1972	3.4
1973	8.8
1974	12.2
1975	7.0
1976	4.8
1977	6.8

In short, these data suggest substantial nominal wage increases for older workers, roughly consistent, on average, with overall inflation levels.

Wage-Tenure Profiles from the Current Population Survey

To estimate wage-tenure profiles by industry and occupation group, we matched the May 1979 Supplement to the CPS March 1979 CPS. The May Supplement provides tenure data, while the wage data come from the March tape. We were able to obtain the required wage, age, and tenure information for somewhat over 15,000 persons in the 24 industry-occupation groups distinguished in the BLS-LOB survey. Relevant cell sample sizes, however, were large enough to obtain "reasonable" estimates for only 16 groups, noted below.

After considerable experimentation with two-way tables showing average salary by age and tenure, we elected simply to obtain least-squares estimates of wage rates using the specification

(8) $W = a_0 + a_1 A + a_2 A^2 + b_1 T + b_2 T^2 + cAT$,

where W is the wage rate, A is age, and T is tenure. To estimate wage levels by age for a person who entered a firm at, for example, age 30, we calculated

(9) $W = \hat{a}_0 + \hat{a}_1 A + \hat{a}_2 A^2 + \hat{b}_1(A-30) + \hat{b}_2(A-30)^2 + \hat{c}(A)(A-30)$,

for values of A between 30 and 65.

The estimated profiles for the total group, and by occupation over all industry groups, are presented in figure 3.1. These profiles are empirical counterparts of the "merit" scale used in the illustrative calculations in chapter 1.

The cross-sectional age-earnings profile (9) for all groups combined increases by about 50 percent between age 30 and age 52 when it reaches its maximum. Then it declines by about 10 percent over

FIGURE 3.1 – Estimated real wage-tenure profiles by age.

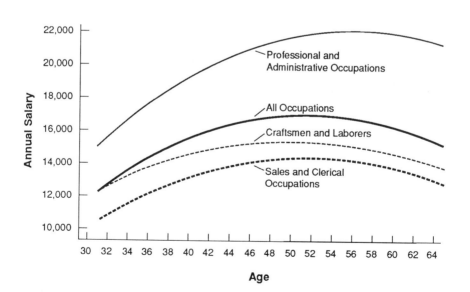

the next 13 years, or about .8 percent per year on average. Assuming a wage inflation rate of 6 percent, therefore, produces a nominal wage rate for older workers increasing at about 5 percent per year. For older workers this path of nominal wage growth seems to be in rough accord with the evidence from the Retirement History Survey. In the calculations of this and the following chapter we assume a 6 percent nominal wage growth through age 65, after which nominal wage growth is assessed to be zero.

In addition to the graphs of the cross-section wage profiles, summary indicators of their shapes are provided in table 3.4. It shows salary at age 30, maximum salary, the age of maximum salary, and salary at age 65, together with average percent increases between the end points and the maximum.

The Decline in Pension Wealth Accrual at Early and Normal Retirement Ages

This section and the following four sections consider earnings-based plans. Earnings-based plans account for approximately 80 percent of the BLS-designated usable plans from the survey and about 65 percent of plans weighted by pension coverage. Each of the earnings-based plans we examine stipulates cliff vesting at 10 years, but the plans have different normal and early retirement ages. Other earnings-based plans with different vesting ages have accrual profiles similar to those we shall describe, but for convenience of exposition we have not included them in this analysis. Of the 1,183 earnings-based plans with 10-year cliff vesting, 508 are integrated with social security under an offset formula.[6]

Average accrual profiles (pension accrual as a ratio of the wage) for the percent of earnings plans with 10-year cliff vesting are shown in appendix table 1 by early and normal retirement ages. These accrual profiles as well as all other accrual profiles discussed in this chapter and the next incorporate a 9 percent nominal interest rate assumption. In forming average accrual profiles, we used the BLS-LOB survey weights; i.e., the average age-accrual profiles on weighted averages of accrual rates at each age. Three of these average profiles, corresponding to plans with the respective early and

38

Table 3.4
Summary Statistics on Wage Profiles by
Industry and Occupation Group

Industry and occupation	Salary at age 30	Max. salary (age)		Salary at age 65	Average % increase age 30 to maximum	Average % decrease maximum to age 65
All	11848	17022	(52)	15216	2.0	−0.8
All:						
Professional and administrative	14470	22232	(57)	21454	2.0	−0.4
Sales and clerical	10112	14446	(52)	12890	1.9	−0.8
Craftsmen and laborers	12228	15366	(51)	13866	1.2	−0.7
Mining	18062	22676	(65)	22676	0.7	−0.0
Construction	15822	18036	(45)	13678	0.9	−1.2
Manufacturing:						
Professional and administrative	16374	24634	(55)	23150	2.0	−0.6
Sales and clerical	10670	14894	(56)	14380	1.5	−0.4
Craftsmen and laborers	10960	14822	(52)	13294	1.6	−0.8
Transportation:						
Professional and administrative	21466	25230	(65)	25230	0.5	−0.0
Sales and clerical	12284	16806	(48)	13128	2.0	−1.3
Craftsmen and laborers	13938	17630	(64)	17628	0.8	−0.0
Wholesale Trade	12644	18416	(48)	12908	2.5	−1.8
Retail Trade:						
Professional and administrative	11268	18844	(48)	12620	3.7	−1.9
Sales and clerical	8528	11932	(46)	7518	2.5	−1.9
Craftsmen and laborers	10974	13538	(49)	11816	1.2	−0.8
Finance	12072	19552	(59)	19194	2.1	−0.3
Services:						
Professional and administrative	13326	19246	(54)	17936	1.9	−0.6
Sales and clerical	9230	10822	(54)	10514	0.7	−0.3
Craftsmen and laborers	11220	12810	(50)	11950	0.7	−0.4

Source: *Current Population Survey* (May 1979).

FIGURE 3.2 – Weighted average accrual rates for percent of earnings plans with 10-year cliff vesting, for selected early and normal retirement ages.

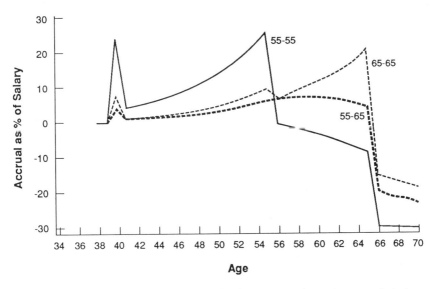

Note: Plans with early or normal retirement supplements are excluded.

normal retirement ages—55–55, 55–65, 65–65—are graphed in figure 3.2. The graphs show very substantial declines in the rate of pension wealth accrual at several critical ages. The first is the age of normal retirement, which equals the age of early retirement for plans with no early retirement option. The postnormal retirement decline in the average rate of accrual primarily reflects (1) the lack of an actuarial or even a nonactuarial increase in benefits in most plans for workers who delay receipt of benefits after normal retirement, and (2) the pre-1986 failure of many plans to credit postnormal retirement service. As mentioned, this second reason for the decline in accrual at normal retirement will be affected by the 1986 Age Discrimination Act that mandates continued participation in the pension benefit formula after the age of normal retirement. A subsection below considers in more detail how credit for postnormal retirement service affects postnormal retirement accrual.

The second sharp decline in the rate of accrual occurs at the age of early retirement, but this decline is substantially lower than the decline at the normal retirement age.[7] The third substantial decline occurs between ages 65 and 66, no matter what the ages of early and normal retirement.

The declines in average accrual rates at these critical ages indicated in appendix table 1, are highlighted in table 3.5. The ages of early and normal retirement are identical in the table. Columns 1, 4, 6, and 8 consider respective retirement ages of 55, 60, 62, and 65. At these ages the accrual rate as a percent of wages declines from .26 to 0, .27 to $-.06$, .25 to $-.13$, and .21 to $-.19$ respectively. Thus, at these ages total annual compensation (wage plus pension accrual) from working declines by 21 percent, 26 percent, 30 percent, and 33 percent respectively. Surely the incentive to continue work with the current employer beyond these ages is very substantially reduced.

In instances where early and normal retirement ages do not coincide, there is also a very substantial decline in the average ratio of pension accrual to the wage at the age of normal retirement. For example, among plans with early retirement at 55 and normal retirement at 60, the average decline is from .14 to $-.09$. There is also a decline at the age of early retirement for these plans, although it is considerably less than the decline at the age of normal retirement. For example, of plans with early retirement at 55 and normal retirement at 65, the average decline at 55 is from .10 to .07, while at 65 the average decline is from .04 to $-.15$.

Finally, consider the substantial decline in the rate of pension accrual between ages 65 and 66. The effective reduction in compensation ranges from 8 percent to 40 percent of the wage rate except for plans with early and normal retirement at 60, in which case the decline is from $-.12$ to $-.14$. Thus, while the stipulations of plans vary tremendously, on average they seem to provide a substantial inducement to retirement after age 65, no matter what the inducement before this age.

Figure 3.2 and table 3.5 also show a large variation in average pension accrual at 40, the age of cliff vesting. It is highest, on av-

Table 3.5
Weighted Average Accrual Rates at Selected Ages
for Percent Earnings Plans with 10-Year Cliff Vesting,
by Early and Normal Retirement Age

Age	Early and Normal Retirement Age							
	(1)	(2)	(3)	(4)	(5)	(6)	(7)	(8)
	55	55	55	60	60	62	62	65
	55	60	65	60	65	62	65	65
40	.244	.111	.071	.034	.047	.038	.054	.036
55	.261	.130	.097					
56	−.003	.100	.068					
60		.143		.269	.167			
61		−.090		−.061	.113			
62						.248	.066	
63						−.130	.017	
65	−.085	−.094	.044	−.121	.112	−.144	.006	.211
66	−.292	−.169	−.152	−.138	−.088	−.266	−.081	−.194
70	−.297	−.184	−.186	−.196	−.182	−.255	−.077	−.234
65–66	20	8	19	2	20	12	8	40

Source: Appendix table 1.

erage, for plans with early and normal retirement at 55 and lowest, on average, for plans with early and normal retirement at 65. As mentioned, because the early retirement reduction is typically less than actuarially fair, pension wealth is generally greatest if benefits are taken at the age of early retirement. Thus the accrued wealth at the age of vesting is usually calculated by discounting benefits from the age of early retirement, assuming that the worker could begin to collect benefits at that age. Figure 3.2, for example, shows a vesting spike of almost 25 percent of earnings for 55–55 plans, 7 percent of earnings for 55–65 plans, and about 4 percent of earnings for 65–65 plans.

In summary, continuation in the labor force after the age of normal retirement, and sometimes early retirement, typically involves a substantial reduction in compensation because of the very large declines in the rate of pension wealth accrual. After the age of 65, there is, on average, a substantial loss in pension accrual, no matter what the ages of early and normal retirement. And the sharp changes in average pension accrual at particular ages provide rather strong *prima facie* evidence against annual spot market clearing; neither wages nor marginal products appear to adjust at these critical ages to meet the spot market equilibrium condition.

Variation Among Plans

Even among plans with the same early and normal retirement ages there is wide variation in accrual rates at each age, particularly after the age of early retirement. To demonstrate this fact, average accrual rates for the 513 plans of appendix table 1 with early retirement at 55 and normal retirement at 65, together with median, maximum, minimum and upper and lower 5 percentile levels, are shown in appendix table 2. The lower 5 percentile points for any age group is that accrual rate such that 5 percent of plans have accruals below that level. The upper 5 percentile point is defined analogously.

Consider the accrual ratio at vesting. While the average vesting ratio for this sample is .071, the median is .021, the maximum is .383, and the minimum is 0. The ratio at the lowest 5th percentile is 0, while it is .201 for the highest 5th percentile. A similarly large dispersion in annual accrual ratios is indicated at each of the ages 40 through 70. Weighted average accrual rates together with upper and lower 5 percentile levels are graphed in figure 3.3. While the average accrual rates between ages 55 and 65 are positive, for many plans the rates prior to age 65 are negative and sizeable. *Thus it is very important not to base judgments about the labor force partici-*

FIGURE 3.3 – Weighted average accrual rates and upper and lower levels for percent of earnings plans with 10-year cliff vesting, early retirement at 55 and normal retirement at 65.

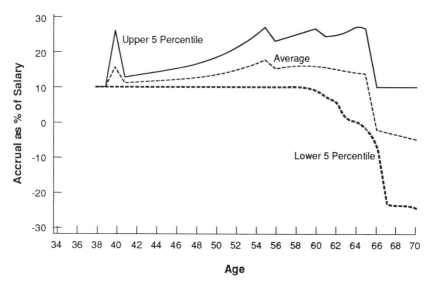

Note: Plans with early or normal retirement supplements are excluded.

pation incentive effects of pensions simply on the basis of average accrual rates.

Additional evidence of the variability of pension accrual profiles is obtained by comparing profiles of particular plans. Figure 3.4 plots the accrual profiles of 4 of the sample's 30 largest plans. Plan 1 exhibits a 29 percent vesting spike, a reduction of 30 percentage points in the accrual ratio at age 55 and a further major reduction at age 65 from $-.063$ to $-.351$. In contrast the vesting spike is only 4 percent for plan 2 in the figure. This plan also exhibits no major reduction in the accrual ratio at early retirement and only a minor reduction at normal retirement. Plan 3's vesting spike is much less than that of plan 1, but the drop off of the accrual ratio at age 55 is very much larger than that in plan 1. This plan also exhibits extremely sharp changes in accrual ratios at ages 60, and 63. Plan 4 exhibits even greater discontinuities in the accrual profile.

FIGURE 3.4 – Accrual profiles for four large plans.

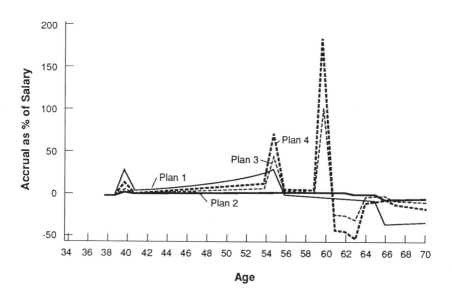

Thus the plans' incentive effects on labor force participation also vary widely.

The Effect of Social Security Offsets

As described above, a substantial number of plans have social security offset provisions, under which pension benefits are reduced by an amount depending upon the recipients' social security benefits. The offset provisions vary widely among plans. In some instances the offset is enough to completely eliminate payment of pension benefits from the private pension plan. Typically, private pension benefit payments are substantially lower with than without the offset provision.

Accrual rates for percent of earning plans with 10-year cliff vesting and early retirement at 55 are shown in appendix table 3 for selected normal retirement ages, with and without social security

FIGURE 3.5 – Weighted average accrual rates for percent of earnings plans with 10-year cliff vesting, early retirement at 55 and normal retirement at 62, for plans with and without social security offsets.

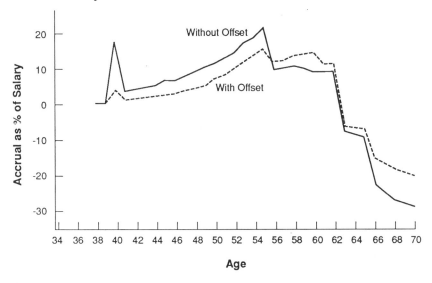

Note: Plans with early or normal retirement supplements are excluded.

offset provisions. The average profiles for offset and nonoffset plans with early retirement at 55 and normal retirement at 62 are graphed in figure 3.5. A noticeable difference between the two groups of plans is the relatively large spike at vesting for plans without the offset compared with the low rate of accrual at vesting for plans with the social security offset. In addition, the accrual ratio at 55 is larger for plans without the offset than for plans with it, and the drop in the rate of accrual is substantially larger for plans without than for plans with the offset. The accrual ratio for plans without an offset is .21 at 55 and drops by almost 60 percent to .09 at 56. In contrast the accrual rate for plans with an offset is about 16 percent at 55 and drops by only about 26 percent to .12 at age 56.

Both groups of plans show negative accrual rates after the age of normal retirement, 62, and both groups of plans show much larger negative accrual rates after 65. Appendix table 3 indicates that the relative accrual rates of the two groups of plans with different normal retirement ages are similar to those shown in the figure.

The table also shows that pension accrual at the age of vesting is rather substantial for plans without a social security offset even among plans with normal retirement at 65. The average accrual rate at vesting for all plans with early retirement at 55 and normal retirement at 65 is .071, as shown in appendix table 1. As indicated in appendix table 3 accrual is over 12 percent for plans without a social security offset, while it is less than 2 percent for plans with an offset.

Postnormal-Retirement Provisions and Pension Accrual

Accrual ratios for percent of earnings plans with early retirement at 55 are shown in table 3.6 for selected normal retirement ages and for alternative postnormal retirement provisions. The postnormal retirement provisions have been grouped into five categories:

(1) Full Credit, Deferred: plans providing full credit according to the standard formula for years worked past the age of normal retirement, but with benefits beginning only after retirement.

(2) No Credit, Deferred: plans with no credit given for work after the age of normal retirement and with benefits beginning only after retirement.

(3) No Credit, Immediate Payout or Actuarial Increase: plans with no credit given for additional work after the age of normal retirement, but with benefits beginning immediately or increased actuarially until benefits are taken.

(4) Limited Credit, Deferred: plans with limited credit given for work after the age of normal retirement or with full credit for service postnormal retirement up to a specified age or number of years; benefits are deferred in these plans until retirement.

(5) Limited Credit, Immediate Payout or Actuarial Increase: plans with provisions analogous to the third category above, but with limited credit rather than no credit.

With the exception of type (3) plans, these provisions typically lead to very negative accrual ratios after the age of normal retirement. Appendix table 4 compares accrual ratios across these 5 types of

47

Table 3.6
Weighted Average Accrual Rates at Critical Ages for Percent of Earnings Plans with 10-Year Cliff Vesting and Early Retirement at 55, Early and Normal Retirement Ages and Industry

Normal Retire.	55			62					65				
Provision	Full credit, Defer.	No credit, Defer.	Limited credit, Defer.	Full credit, Defer.	No credit, Defer.	No credit, Immed. payout or Actuarial increase	Limited credit, Defer.	Limited credit, Immed. payout or Actuarial increase	Full credit, Defer.	No credit, Defer.	No credit, Immed. payout or Actuarial increase	Limited credit, Defer.	Limited credit, Immed. payout or Actuarial increase
No. of Plans	18	5	129	76	7	2	66	35	212	207	63	22	9
Age													
55	.244	.084	.261	.191	.190	.250	.170	.161	.105	.081	.077	.112	.116
56	.015	−.080	−.007	.119	.137	.091	.058	.094	.071	.051	.062	.097	.112
62				.082	.216	−.091	.094	.066					
63				−.064	−.378	0	−.033	−.051					
65									.027	.041	.080	.041	.037

Source: Appendix table 7

plans with varying postnormal retirement benefit provisions. The table examines plans with alternative normal retirement ages, but all with early retirement occurring at 55. Accrual rates at critical ages are shown in table 3.6. The figures are somewhat surprising, indicating quite negative accrual ratios even for plans that fully credit postnormal retirement service; indeed, in certain cases, these negative accrual ratios are larger in absolute value than negative accrual ratios of plans that provide no credit. The accrual rates are affected not only by the plan provisions, but also by wage growth and by life expectancy. With fewer years to live, pension wealth can decline even if the benefit, upon receipt, is larger.

To isolate the impact of the choice of retirement provisions, accrual ratios for percent of earnings plans with early retirement at 55 and selected normal retirement ages are calculated, first assuming that all of the plans had a full credit provision, and second assuming that all the plans had no credit provision. These results are shown in table 3.7. The table indicates that the effect of crediting service after normal retirement depends importantly on the age of normal retirement. For plans with a normal retirement age of 55, negative accrual ratios are larger in absolute value under no crediting prior to age 66 and smaller in absolute value thereafter. In part, the differences reflect lower wage growth as workers age. Full credit incorporates credit for additional years of service, but also the effect of wage change.

Early and Normal Retirement Supplements

Approximately 11.4 percent of plans have early and 7.5 have normal retirement supplements. The typical normal retirement supplement provides an addition to otherwise calculated benefits if the individual postpones retirement until the normal retirement age. The typical early retirement supplement provides an addition to benefits if retirement occurs after the age of early retirement.

The average accrual rates for percent of earnings and flat plans with supplements, with 10-year cliff vesting, and with early and normal retirement at 55 and 65 respectively, are shown in table 3.8 by type of supplement. There are only two plans in the category with

Table 3.7

Weighted Average Accrual Rates for Percent of Earnings Plans With 10-Year Cliff Vesting and Early Retirement at 55, by Normal Retirement Age, *Assuming* Full Credit and No Credit Postretirement Provisions

Normal Ret.	55		62		65	
Assumed Post-Normal Ret. Provision	Full Credit	No Credit	Full Credit	No Credit	Full Credit	No Credit
No. of Plans	152	152	187	187	513	513
Age						
40	.244	.244	.106	.106	.071	.071
41	.045	.045	.023	.023	.013	.013
54	.231	.231	.160	.160	.083	.083
55	.261	.261	.185	.185	.097	.097
56	−.002	−.244	.102	.102	.068	.068
57	−.011	−.229	.105	.105	.072	.072
58	−.019	−.215	.118	.118	.076	.076
59	−.027	−.202	.117	.117	.077	.077
60	−.037	−.139	.114	.114	.079	.079
61	−.049	−.178	.099	.099	.068	.068
62	−.059	−.167	.098	.098	.064	.064
63	−.068	−.157	−.060	−.284	.056	.056
64	−.077	−.148	−.069	−.267	.053	.063
65	−.086	−.139	−.079	−.252	.044	.044
66	−.133	−.130	−.150	−.237	−.132	−.225
67	−.177	−.128	−.192	−.233	−.153	−.222
68	−.219	−.127	−.231	−.232	−.172	−.219
69	−.261	−.124	−.260	−.227	−.190	−.216
70	−.301	−.123	−.285	−.223	−.205	−.212

Table 3.8
Weighted Average Accrual Rates at Selected Ages for Percent of Earnings and Flat Plans with 10-Year Cliff Vesting, Early and Normal Retirement at 55–65, and Early or Normal Retirement Supplement, by Type of Supplement

	Type of Supplement		
	Normal	Early	Both
No. of Plans	2	10	10
Age			
40	.065	.111	.035
41	.012	.197	.009
54	.057	.121	.108
55	.065	.442	.621
56	.047	−.0007	−.051
57	.051	−.008	−.049
58	.054	−.014	−.043
59	.058	−.022	−.046
60	.061	−.011	−.051
61	.066	−.049	−.068
62	.070	−.058	−.072
63	.074	−.073	−.080
64	.078	−.022	.009
65	.601	−.031	.008
66	−.181	−.247	−.092
67	−.180	−.213	−.167
68	−.179	−.207	−.164
69	−.179	−.204	−.163
70	−.178	−.201	−.160

only normal retirement supplements, but, nonetheless, the effect of the supplements can be seen in the first column of the table. The accrual rate jumps from about 8 percent of the wage at age 64, to 60 percent of the wage at age 65. Thus the supplement apparently provides a relatively strong incentive to remain with the firm until age 65, but thereafter there is a sharp drop in the accrual rate to −18 percent.

Accrual rates for plans with early retirement supplements are shown in the second column of the table. In this case there is a sharp increase in the accrual rate from .12 at age 54 to .44 at age 55, with a sharp drop thereafter. Again, the provision seems to provide a substantial incentive to remain with the firm to the age of early retirement, with a very substantial decline thereafter. Accrual rates for plans with both types of supplement are shown in the last column of the table. In this case there is a rather large spike at the age of early retirement, equal to 62 percent of the wage in that year, with a smaller, but still noticeable spike at about the age of normal retirement.

Accrual rates for percent of earnings and flat plans with either type of supplement are shown in appendix table 5 for selected early and normal retirement ages. The spikes in the accrual rates are highlighted with dashed lines. Consider, for example, plans with early retirement at age 55. The spike created by the early retirement supplement is from .22 to .39 for plans with normal retirement at 55, from .12 to .50 for plans with normal retirement at 60, and from .11 to .48 for plans with normal retirement at 65. Of the 56 plans with normal retirement at age 60, the pension accrual rate at that age is on average equivalent to 100 percent of the wage rate.

Similar discontinuities in the accrual ratios are evident for plans with other early and normal retirement ages. For example, of plans with early and normal retirement at age 60, the accrual rate at that age is equivalent to 64 percent of the annual wage for persons aged 60. Thus these special supplements create very significant one-time additions to pension wealth and, therefore, provide very important incentives to remain with the firm until the age that the special supplement is awarded. The special supplements also further dramatize the wide variation in the incentive effects implicit in the provisions of private pension plans.

Flat Benefit Plans

Accrual ratios for flat benefit plans with selected early and normal retirement are shown in appendix table 6. This table can be compared to appendix table 1 which presents comparable numbers for percent of earnings plans. The accrual profiles for flat plans with early-normal retirement at ages 55–55, 55–60, 55–65 are shown graphically in figure 3.6. In general, the accrual profiles for the flat benefit plans look quite similar to those for percent of earnings plans. Recall that we have assumed that the flat benefit increases with the rate of inflation, assumed to be 6 percent annually in our calculations. While it is not possible to make comparisons for plans

FIGURE 3.6 – Weighted average accrual rates for flat rate plans with 10-year cliff vesting, for selected early and normal retirement ages.

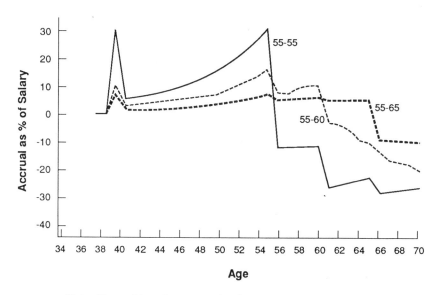

Note: Plans with early or normal retirement supplements are excluded.

with each of the early and normal retirement combinations because of the relatively small sample sizes, for several early-normal retirement age combinations there are rather large numbers of plans of both types, e.g., the combinations 55–60, 55–65, and 60–65. The average decline in the accrual ratio between the age of early retirement to age 66 is .30 for percent of earnings plans versus .39 for flat benefits plans in the case of the 55–60 retirement age combination. It is .25 versus .16 for the 55–65 combination, and .26 versus .17 for the 60–65 combination.

Average accrual ratios at several critical ages for plans with early retirement at 55 and normal retirement at 65 are shown below for percent of earnings and flat benefit plans:

Age	Percent of Earnings Plans	Flat Plans
40	.071	.070
55	.097	.073
56	.068	.052
65	.044	.049
66	−.152	−.091
70	−.186	−.102

The accrual rates for these plans at all ages are graphed in figure 3.7. The evidence indicates that the two types of plan provide rather similar incentive effects.

The provisions of flat rate plans, like those of percent of earnings plans, also yield widely differing ratios, even among plans with the same early and normal retirement ages. Indications of the dispersion of the accrual ratios among flat plans with early and normal retirement at 55 and 65 respectively are shown in appendix table 7. While the average accrual rate at age 55, for example, is 7 percent, the minimum value is 0 and the maximum 24 percent. Similarly at age 56, while the average is about 5 percent, the maximum is 20 percent, and the minimum is about 0. At 65, the average is 5 percent, with a maximum of almost 33 percent and a minimum of about −20 percent. At 66, after the age of normal retirement, the average accrual rate is −9 percent, while the minimum is −56 percent and the maximum 0. Thus the incentive for retirement varies widely among flat benefit, as well as percent of earnings plans.

FIGURE 3.7 – Weighted average accrual rates for percent of earnings and flat rate plans with 10-year cliff vesting, early retirement at 55 and normal retirement at 65.

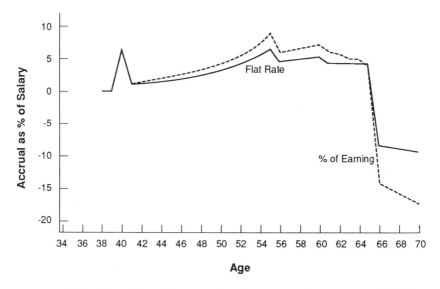

Note: Plans with early or normal retirement supplements are excluded.

Summary

This chapter has presented ratios of pension benefit accrual to wage earnings for a wide range of U.S. defined benefit pension plans. Typical plan provisions provide a strong incentive for retirement after the age of plan normal retirement, and a large proportion of plans provide a strong incentive for retirement after the age of early retirement. A striking feature of the incentive effects of pension plans is their wide variation across plans. For example, while the average plan may provide reduced, but still positive, accrual after the age of early retirement, for a large proportion of plans the accrual rate after this age is a sizeable negative number. Thus it would not be unusual for the reduction in pension benefit accrual after the age of early retirement to be equivalent to a 30 percent reduction in wage earnings. The accrual rate at the age of vesting can range from as low as 2 percent of wage earnings in that year to as high as 100 percent of wage earnings, depending upon the plan type and on the age of initial employment. Thus for some employees, vesting can be a very important determinant of job change decisions.

Special early and normal retirement supplements also add very substantially to accrued pension wealth at particular ages and thus encourage workers to remain with a firm until these benefits are received. The accrual profiles under flat benefit plans are very similar to the profiles under percent of earnings plans, if one assumes that the flat benefit is increased to keep pace with the rate of inflation.

The evidence from a broad range of pension plans suggests the possibility that the rapid increase in pension plan coverage over the past two or three decades could have contributed very substantially to the reduction in the labor force participation of older workers during this period. The plans may also have an important effect on labor mobility.

4

The Pension Cost of Job Change and Sex, Industry, and Occupation Differences in Accrual

This chapter considers two issues. First is the question of the costs of job change in terms of reduced pension benefits. The second concerns how pensions contribute to compensation differentials between males and females, between workers in different industries, and between workers in different occupations.

Cost of Changing to a No-Pension Job

There are many ways to think about the effect of job change on pension accrual and the potential incentive effects of pension provisions on the job change decision. One approach is to consider the effect of job change on accrued pension wealth at the age of retirement, say the age of normal retirement. Another way is to consider the expected loss in future pension wealth from changing jobs as a proportion of expected future wages. We consider both measures.

Consider a person who starts a job at some age, say 31. Suppose that at a given subsequent age the person could change to another job and obtain the same future wages as on the current job. Suppose his options are either to stay on the current job until normal retirement or to switch to the second job and stay on that one until the age of normal retirement. But suppose that the new job has no pension. Then the loss in pension wealth is equal to the pension wealth that the worker would accrue if he were to stay with the current employer until the age of normal retirement. In other words, the loss is the proportion of *future* compensation, on the current job, that is in the form of pension benefits. This projected pension compensation measure differs from the accrued vested benefits measure examined above; it projects what the worker will accrue in benefits if he stays

57

with the firm through normal retirement in contrast to the accrued vested benefits, which indicates what vested benefits the worker has accrued to date. The loss in projected benefits from job change relative to the present value of expected future wages is shown in appendix tables 8, 9, and 10. These tables are all usable earnings-based as well as flat benefit plans.

Appendix table 8 assumes that an individual begins employment with the first firm at age 31. Appendix table 9 assumes a starting age of 41, and appendix table 10 a starting age of 51. The tables present these projected benefit-loss ratios by plan normal retirement age, and loss ratios are calculated through the age of normal retirement. To obtain a more concise picture of the losses, they are shown for selected ages of job change in table 4.1. Note that there are no vesting spikes in these tables since we are considering projected, rather than accrued vested benefits. For plans with normal retirement at 65, the loss in pension wealth relative to expected wages is relatively small, between 4 and 6 percent for all ages of job change, with the exception of job change at age 59 when joining the firm at age 51. In the latter case, the remaining working life of the individual is short, and he is not yet vested. Thus the loss in potential pension accrual is relatively large compared to future earnings.

Among plans with earlier normal retirement—55, 60, or 62—the potential loss in future pension accrual is considerably larger, typically on the order of 8 to 20 percent of future earnings. The loss if one changes jobs just before normal retirement, however, is, in some instances, much larger than this, as high as 30 to 50 percent. For example, if at age 31 one enters a plan with normal retirement at age 60, the loss ratio if one changes jobs at 59 is 31 percent. If the individual enters at 51 and leaves at 59, the loss is almost 50 percent.

The greater relative loss with earlier normal retirement is shown in figure 4.1, which presents loss ratios versus age for plans with normal retirement at 55 and at 65, starting at age 31. Recall that the loss ratios indicate that at any age future pension accrual is a larger proportion of compensation with younger ages of normal retirement. Basically, this is because benefits will be collected over more retire-

Table 4.1

Loss in Expected Pension Wealth if Change to No-Pension Job, as Percent of Expected Wages by Age of Job Change, Age of Starting Job, and Age of Normal Retirement[a]

Starting Age and Age of Job Change	Plan Normal Retirement			
	55	60	62	65
31:				
44	.13	.10	.08	.04
49	.16	.14	.09	.05
54	.12	.18	.09	.05
59	--	.31	.06	.04
41:				
44	.10	.08	.08	.04
49	.19	.12	.11	.06
54	.10	.11	.15	.05
59	--	.09	.13	.05
51:				
44	--	--	--	--
49	--	--	--	--
54	--	.12	.13	.06
59	--	.48	.33	.12

Source: Appendix tables 11, 12, 13.

a. With expectations evaluated to plan normal retirement age.

FIGURE 4.1 – Loss in expected pension wealth if change to no-pension job, as a percent of expected wages, for normal retirement at 55 versus 65.

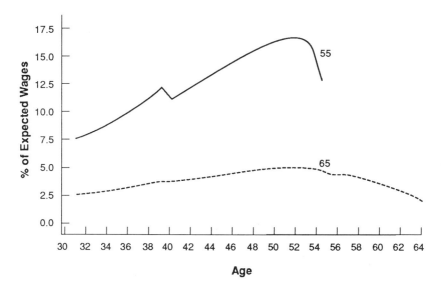

ment years. The comparisons reflect possible differences in age-wage profiles, due to different industry and occupation mixes, but do not match individual plan provisions and wage profiles.

The effect of starting age is shown graphically in figure 4.2 for plans with normal retirement at 60. The graphs and table 4.1 make clear that there is no simple relationship between the pension proportion of future compensation and the age of hire. The proportion is unusually high, however, for persons hired at 51.

A limiting case of numbers like those presented in table 4.1 is the present discounted value of expected pension benefits at the age of hire as a proportion of expected future wages at that time. These numbers, of course, indicate the cost to the employer of pension benefits versus wages if a person stays with the employer from the time of hire to the age of early or normal retirement. Such ratios are presented in table 4.2 by age of initial employment and plan normal retirement age. The ratios are presented first assuming that the individual remains with the firm until the age of early retirement and

FIGURE 4.2 – Loss in expected pension wealth if change to no-pension job, as a percent of expected wages, for normal retirement at 60, by age started job.

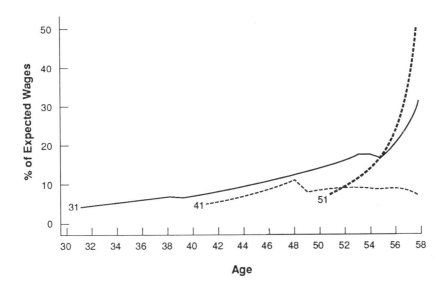

then assuming that the person remains until the age of normal retirement. It can be seen from the table that the present discounted value of pension versus wage compensation is small on average, ranging from about 2 percent to about 10 percent. The average proportion of compensation in pension benefits is typically larger the later the age of initial employment. For example, the ratio of pension benefits to wages for plans with normal retirement at 62 is .049 if one enters the firm at 31 and stays to the age of normal retirement. The ratio is .062 if one enters at 41, and .094 if one enters at 51. To the extent that this is true, pension provisions may mitigate against hiring older workers, unless their wages at subsequent ages are lower than those of workers of the same age but hired at younger ages. It is important to understand that while these ratios may appear relatively small, the pattern of pension accrual may still have a very substantial effect on labor force participation, as demonstrated below and as the analysis above suggests.

Table 4.2

**Present Discounted Value of Expected Pension Benefits as a
Proportion of Expected Wages, at Age of Hire, by Age of Hire
and Plan Normal Retirement Age**

Age of Hire and Plan Normal Retirement Age	If Retire at Early Retirement Age	If Retire at Normal Retirement Age
31:		
All	.038	.044
55	.072	.072
60	.044	.055
62	.043	.049
65	.022	.026
41:		
All	.042	.049
55	.078	.079
60	.060	.064
62	.051	.062
65	.027	.034
51:		
All	.045	.060
55	---	---
60	.069	.080
62	.054	.094
65	.039	.046

The most striking feature of these loss ratios is the wide variation among plans. To demonstrate the dispersion, the mean loss ratio together with the minimum and maximum at each age of job change are shown in table 4.3 for plans with normal retirement at 65 and for persons who enter the firm at age 31. Up to age 55—which is the age of early retirement for a substantial proportion of plans—the loss is close to zero for some plans and indeed is even negative for some. For other plans, however, the loss is very high, ranging up to 26 percent of future earnings at age 54. After 55, the maximum loss is typically over 30 percent, while the minimum is close to −20 percent at each age. Pension accrual after the age of early retirement

Table 4.3

Dispersion of Loss in Expected Pension Wealth if Change to No-Pension Job, for Plans in Table 4.7 With Normal Retirement at Age 65

Age	Mean	Minimum	Maximum
31	.026	0	.098
40	.035	−.010	.139
41	.037	−.009	.145
50	.049	−.012	.219
51	.050	−.022	.229
52	.050	−.034	.240
54	.048	−.068	.264
55	.044	−.182	.276
56	.043	−.181	.289
63	.023	−.248	.321
64	.016	−.220	.367
65			

is negative in many instances. For a member of such a plan, it would pay to leave this firm, taking early retirement benefits, and join another firm, assuming that one could join the second firm and obtain the same expected future wages. These data again demonstrate the very wide variation in the incentive effects inherent in pension plan provisions.

Job Change and Pension Wealth at Age of Normal Retirement

Pension wealth at the age of normal retirement (as opposed to the age of job change) may be reduced very substantially by job change, as shown in table 4.4. A person who began work at 31 and changed to another job at 41 would have accrued, on average, only 72 percent of the pension wealth of a person who began at 31 and remained in the same firm. If he changed jobs at 41 and again at 51, he would accrue only 43 percent of the pension wealth of a person with no job change. This percent ranges from a low of 30 on average in transportation to 60 percent in construction. Thus the loss in pension wealth with job change seems to provide a potentially large incentive against job mobility.

Because some plans place a limit on years of service that are credited in calculating benefits, it may in some instances pay to change jobs and begin to accrue benefits in a new plan. This leads to ratios that are greater than one in a few instances. The minimum and maximum values over all industries arise in anomalous plans, and these should not be given much weight; but they do suggest that there is substantial variation among plans in this respect, as well as in other respects discussed above.

Pension Accrual Ratios and Age of Initial Employment

Vested pension accrual rates for percent of earnings plans with 10-year cliff vesting are shown in appendix tables 11 and 12 for persons beginning employment at ages 41 and 51 respectively. The tables are analogous to appendix table 1, presenting information by plan for early and normal retirement ages. To provide an easier comparison of the accrual rates by starting age, accrual rates for

Table 4.4
Weighted Average Pension Wealth (or Ratio) at Normal Retirement, by Age of Initial Employment, and by Job Change, and by Industry: All Plans

Industry and No. of Plans		Age of Initial Employment			Pension Wealth at Normal Retirement Relative to Wealth Without Job Change if:		
		31	41	51	Change at 41	Change at 51	Change at 41 and 51
All industries	2342	32491	21410	10924	.72	.85	.43
Minimum		0	0	0	0	0	0
Maximum		197070	175899	117291	4.97	8.18	5.09
Mining	39	44856	27237	13147	.62	.81	.38
Construction	9	35778	28680	16837	.87	1.02	.60
Manufacturing	1297	31448	20393	10633	.73	.85	.44
Transportation	328	38680	22350	8598	.57	.81	.30
Wholesale trade	100	30836	21989	13135	.74	.87	.50
Retail trade	260	19453	13002	6024	.67	.80	.41
Finance	7	38864	30766	17309	.91	1.01	.58
Services	8	29993	22551	12520	.77	.87	.47

selected ages are shown in table 4.5. Accrual ratios for plans with early and normal retirement at 55 and 65, respectively, are graphed in figure 4.3.

The accrual rate at vesting is the most important difference across initial employment ages. For example, as shown in table 4.5, the accrual rate at vesting is .24 for persons beginning employment at 31; it is .62 for those beginning at age 41 and .92 for those beginning at age 51. The difference is simply due to the fact that the later the age of initial employment, the nearer is the time of benefit receipt at the age of vesting. The accrual rate at vesting increases with age of initial employment for each early-normal retirement age category. Otherwise, the pattern of accrual rates does not vary by starting age, except that the absolute value of the rates, both positive and negative, is smaller as the age of initial employment increases. Again, this is simply because potential benefits are lower with later starting

FIGURE 4.3 – Weighted average accrual rates for percent of earnings plans with 10-year cliff vesting, early retirement at 55 and normal retirement at 65, by age started job.

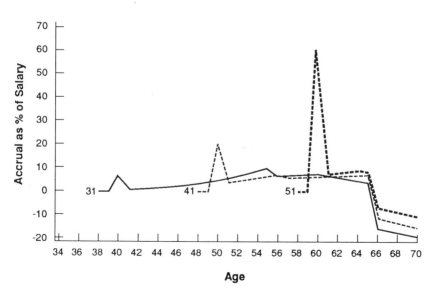

Note: Plans with early or normal retirement supplements are excluded.

Table 4.5

Pension Accrual Rates for Percent of Earnings Plans with 10-Year Cliff Vesting, by Early and Normal Retirement Age and by Age of Initial Employment, for Selected Ages

Starting Age and Age	Early-Normal Retirement							
	55 55	55 60	55 65	60 60	60 65	62 62	62 65	65 65
31:								
40	.24	.11	.07	.03	.05	.04	.05	.04
50	.14	.08	.05	.07	.03	.07	.02	.03
55	.26	.13	.10	.15	.08	.13	.04	.07
60	−.04	.14	.08	.27	.17	.24	.05	.12
62	−.06	−.09	.06	−.09	.12	.25	.07	.15
65	−.09	−.09	.04	−.12	.11	−.14	.01	.21
66	−.29	−.17	−.15	−.14	−.09	−.27	−.08	−.19
41:								
40	0	0	0	0	0	0	0	0
50	.62	.35	.21	.35	.13	.02	.14	.13
55	.18	.13	.07	.11	.05	.10	.03	.05
60	−.01	.12	.07	.21	.10	.18	.06	.12
62	−.02	−.00	.07	−.02	.08	.22	.07	.14
65	−.04	−.02	.07	−.04	.08	−.04	.03	.20
66	−.12	−.12	−.11	−.19	−.06	−.19	−.08	−.12
51:								
40	0	0	0	0	0	0	0	0
50	0	0	0	0	0	0	0	0
55	0	0	0	0	0	0	0	0
60	.92	.77	.61	1.04	.45	.64	.54	.45
62	.04	.03	.08	.03	.06	.17	.10	.10
65	.02	.01	.08	.01	.07	.03	.08	.15
66	−.10	−.05	−.08	−.04	−.04	−.06	−.08	−.07

Source: Appendix tables 1, 14, and 15.

ages and, thus, potential losses after the age of early or normal retirement are smaller.

Notice that the accrual rate after the age of 65 is negative in each case. Plan provisions typically make the age of early and normal retirement dependent upon age and years of service. Thus, in practice, the ages of early and normal retirement are typically somewhat higher for persons beginning employment at age 51. But in no case is the age of normal retirement greater than 65.

Pension Accrual Rates and Pension Cost by Sex

Because women on average live longer than men, women will typically receive pension benefits longer than men. We consider here the effect of this difference in life expectancy on pension accrual and the value of pension benefits. The weighted average of the accrued benefits of women versus the accrued benefits of men by age are shown in table 4.6 for all plans in the sample. At the most common vesting age, 10 years, the ratio is about 1.08, so that women's vested benefits are approximately 8 percent higher than men's. The ratio increases gradually to about 1.10 at age 60 and about 1.13 at 65. If otherwise identical men and women were to work until age 70, the average ratio would be 1.17. The ratios do not vary significantly by early and normal retirement age, and thus a breakdown by plan type is not presented.

Accrual Ratios by Industry and Occupation

Industry

Average accrual profiles for selected industries are shown in appendix table 13. For purposes of comparison and for ease of exposition, profiles are presented only for plans with early retirement at 55, although profiles for three normal retirement ages, 55, 62, 65, are shown. The most apparent difference among industries is in the proportion of plans with particular early and normal retirement ages. For example, in retail trade and services almost all plans have normal retirement at 65, with only a few plans with early retirement at 55 or 62. On the other hand, almost 62 percent of plans in transpor-

Table 4.6
The Ratio of Accrued Pension Benefits of Women vs. Men, by
Age, All Plans[a]

Age	Ratio	Age	Ratio
31	1	51	1.109
32	1	52	1.106
33	1	53	1.103
34	1	54	1.099
35	1.032	55	1.094
36	1.030	56	1.096
37	1.032	57	1.098
38	1.037	58	1.101
39	1.036	59	1.103
40	1.082	60	1.102
41	1.083	61	1.108
42	1.085	62	1.113
43	1.087	63	1.120
44	1.089	64	1.126
45	1.091	65	1.131
46	1.094	66	1.138
47	1.096	67	1.145
48	1.099	68	1.153
49	1.102	69	1.161
50	1.105	70	1.170

a. There are 2342 plans. Starting age is 31.

tation have early and normal retirement at 55, with approximately 20 percent of plans reporting normal retirement at 62 and 20 percent at 65. In manufacturing, 66 percent of plans have normal retirement at 65, 28 percent at 62, and about 6 percent at 55.

Among plans with the same early and normal retirement age, however, appendix table 13 indicates little difference in average accrual profiles across industries. Table 4.7 isolates accrual ratios at critical ages, in particular before and after the age of early retirement and before and after the age of normal retirement. Averages are only presented for cells with more than 10 plans. Two dashes indicate that there were fewer than 10. The cell was left blank if the corresponding age did not represent a critical age for the plan in question. Only in manufacturing and transportation were there a substantial number of plans with early and normal retirement at 55. In these two industries, the accrual profiles look very similar. Three industries had a significant number of plans with early retirement at 55 and normal retirement at 62, and again there seems to be little noticeable difference in accrual patterns among the plans by industry. All industries have plans with normal retirement at 65. But even in this case, the profiles seem quite similar. The only possible exception seems to be retail trade, where pension accrual relative to the wage rate is less generous than in the other industry groups.

Nonetheless, a typical worker apparently faces a much greater incentive to leave the labor force early in some industries than in others. For example, a large proportion of workers covered by pensions in transportation would experience a 27 percent reduction in effective compensation by continuing to work between 55 and 56. While at 55 pension accrual would be equivalent to about 27 percent of wages for many workers in this industry, if the worker continued in the labor force until age 66, his annual loss in pension wealth would be equivalent to 30 percent of wage earnings at 66. A large proportion of workers in manufacturing have plans with early retirement at 55 and normal retirement at 65. In this case, the accrual at 55 averages about 9 percent of the wage at 55 and declines only to about 7 percent of the wage by 65. But then the accrual rate becomes negative, and if the worker were to continue in the labor force

Table 4.7
Weighted Average Accrual Rates at Selected Ages
for Percent of Earnings Plans with 10-Year Cliff Vesting
and Early Retirement at 55, by Early and Normal
Retirement Ages and Industry

Early and Normal Retirement Ages, Age	Industry				
	Manufac-turing	Trans-portation	Retail Trade	Finance	Services
55–55					
40	.227	.257	---	---	---
55	.240	.269	---	---	---
56	−.008	−.003	---	---	---
62					
63					
65	−.099	−.080	---	---	---
66	−.288	−.300	---	---	---
70	−.288	−.302	---	---	---
55–62					
40	.091	.168	---	.086	---
55	.158	.228	---	.250	---
56	.100	.078	---	.141	---
62	.101	.087	---	.044	---
63	−.080	−.077	---	−.093	---
65	−.095	−.097	---	−.108	---
66	−.158	−.242	---	−.187	---
70	−.216	−.329	---	−.251	---
55–65					
40	.056	.122	.080	.077	.068
55	.087	.127	.056	.146	.098
56	.067	.091	.034	.092	.082
62					
63					
65	.068	.058	−.059	.096	.054
66	−.141	−.206	−.156	−.167	−.144
70	−.177	−.246	−.162	−.222	−.169

between 65 and 66, the decline in pension accrual would amount to an effective reduction in compensation of about 21 percent.

Occupation

Among plans with the same early and normal retirement ages, the pension accrual ratios do not differ noticeably by occupation. Accrual ratios for professionals, clerical workers, and production workers are shown in appendix table 14 plans with early retirement at age 55 and three normal retirement ages—55, 62, and 65. Plans in the 55–65 group are graphed by occupation in figure 4.4.

According to the table and the figure, given the age of normal retirement, there is no substantial differences in average accrual ratios by occupational group. Consider, for example, plans with normal retirement at age 55: at age 55, the accrual ratio is .29 for professionals, .25 for clerical workers, and .25 for production workers. At

FIGURE 4.4 – Weighted average accrual rates for percent of earnings plans with 10-year cliff vesting, early retirement at 55 and normal retirement at 65, by occupation.

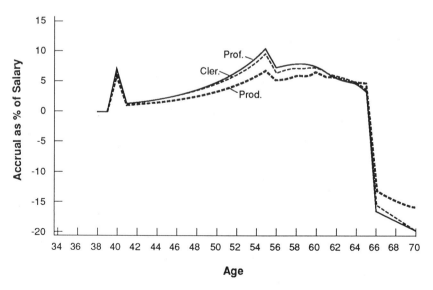

Note: Plans with early or normal retirement supplements are excluded.

age 66, the accrual ratio has dropped to $-.30$ for professionals, $-.30$ for clerical workers, and $-.29$ for production workers. Similarly, close ratios are observed for the other two normal retirement ages. For example, at age 62 the average accrual ratios for plans with normal retirement at 62 are .10 for professionals, .10 for clerical workers, and .10 for production workers. This is not to say that there are no differences in pension accrual by occupational groups. It simply says that conditional on having a plan with given early and normal retirement ages, the accrual ratios for the occupational groups are very similar. The data in appendix table 14 may, however, be concealing intra-industry variation in accrual profiles by occupation for given retirement ages.

To address this potential ambiguity, accrual ratios for the same plans treated in appendix table 14 are presented in appendix table 15, but only for manufacturing. But here again there is very little difference in the accrual profiles by occupation. Consider, for example, the drop in accrual ratios between ages 55 and 66. For plans with normal retirement at age 55, the decline is .58 (.287 minus $-.295$) for professionals, .51 for clerical workers, and .50 for production workers. The corresponding declines are .29 for professionals, .30 for clerical workers, and .35 for production workers, respectively, in plans with normal retirement at 62. Only among plans with normal retirement at age 65 is there a noticeable difference in the accrual ratios by occupation. In this case, the drop between age 55 and age 66 is .29 for professionals, .25 for clerical workers, but somewhat less than .18 for production workers. Thus we conclude that differences in pension accrual ratios by occupation are primarily due to different plan types or to differences in early and normal retirement ages, given the general type of plan. Production workers, for example, are more likely to have flat benefit plans than professionals.

Summary

While the expected loss in pension benefits due to job change is apparently relatively small in many instances, it is rather large in others, and there is wide variation among plans with the loss very high in some cases and, indeed, in other cases there may be a gain to changing jobs. In addition, accrued benefits at the age of retirement are typically much lower with job change than if a person remains on the same job.

Because women typically live longer than men, accrued pension benefits at any age are higher for women than for men, about 13 percent on average at age 65, for example.

Given early and normal retirement ages, there is little difference in plan accrual profiles by industry or by occupation. Differences in pension benefits by industry depend more on the type of plan than on variations among plans with the same basic provisions.

5

Pension Accrual in a Large Firm

The actual relationship between pension accrual and retirement in a large Fortune 500 firm is considered in this chapter and chapter 6. The FIRM data are the employment and earnings histories between 1969 and 1984 of all workers who were employed by the FIRM in any of the years between 1980 and 1984. The provisions of the FIRM's pension plan are such that different workers face very different pension accrual profiles and, thus, pension compensation. As a consequence, different workers face very different incentives for continued work versus retirement. The analysis begins with descriptions of the FIRM's data, its pension plan, and the incentive effects of its pension plan. For purposes of comparison the accrual of social security benefits is described together with pension benefit accrual. The evaluation of the incentive effects of plan provisions requires the estimation of wage earnings. The procedure used to estimate these profiles is described in appendix III. Chapter 6 examines the relationship between wage earnings, pension wealth, and social security accrual, on the one hand, and the age of retirement (more precisely, departure from the FIRM), on the other.

The FIRM's Data

Data are available for each worker employed in the FIRM at any time from the beginning of 1980 through the end of 1984. Most of these workers were in the FIRM in more than one year and many for all years. These years define the sample. Earnings for workers in the sample are available beginning in 1969, if the worker was employed then, or beginning in the year that the person joined the FIRM, if it was after 1969. Thus it is possible to follow the same person for up to 17 years. In particular, it is possible to estimate individual-specific earnings effects. By combining data for workers of different ages and with different years of service in the FIRM, it

75

is possible to predict earnings. We use these predicted earnings, together with pension and social security accrual, to consider the incentive to leave the FIRM.

In addition to the earnings information, the data contain the worker's age, service, sex, and whether he or she is a manager, a salesworker, or an office worker. Unfortunately we only know the worker's current job classification; i.e., we cannot tell whether a worker has changed jobs in the past. We also have no information on health, education, assets, or marital status, all of which may influence the retirement decision.

Plan Provisions

The FIRM has a defined benefit pension plan with earnings-related benefits and a social security offset. The plan's early and normal retirement ages are 55 and 65 respectively with vesting after 10 years. Actuarially reduced benefits are available starting at age 55 for vested terminators—vested workers who leave the FIRM prior to age 55. For early retirees—workers who retire between ages 55 and 65—less than actuarially reduced benefits are provided. For workers who retire after age 65 there is no special actuarial benefit increase.

In addition to the more favorable benefit reduction afforded to early retirees, early retirees receive a supplemental benefit equal to their social security offset between the time they retire and the time they reach age 65. Hence, in comparison to a vested terminator who leaves the FIRM at age 54 and starts collecting benefits at age 55, an early retiree who leaves at age 55 enjoys a smaller benefit reduction and also receives a supplemental benefit until age 65. Not surprisingly, the profile of vested accrued benefits by age jumps sharply for most workers at age 55. Thus there is a large bonus for remaining with the FIRM until age 55.

The formula for the basic benefit before reduction for early retirement and before any applicable social security offset is the average earnings base times 2 percent times the first N years of continuous service (where N lies between 15 and 25), plus 1 percent times the rest of continuous service:

(10)   Benefits = (Earnings Base)   [(.02)(Service)]
            if Service is less than N years
        Benefits = (Earnings Base)   [(.02)(Service) + (.01)(Service − N)]
            if Service is greater than N years.

The average earnings base is calculated based on earnings between the start year and the year of either vested termination or retirement. The start year has traditionally been increased by two years every other year, varying from 7 to 8 years before the current years. In our accrual calculations we assume a one- or two-year increase in the start year every two years. Excluding the two lowest years of earnings (except that the number of earnings years used can't be reduced below five), the earnings base is calculated as the average annual earnings from the start year to the year of vested termination or retirement.

The social security adjustment is a complex service-related function of the social security benefit calculated by the FIRM. The FIRM's calculation of the worker's age 65 social security benefit, is based on the worker's earnings to date with the FIRM. In the social security benefit formula, earnings last year are extrapolated forward, assuming no growth factor, until the worker reaches age 65. The average of past earnings with the FIRM as well as extrapolated future earnings is then entered into a three-bracket progressive benefit formula to arrive at the FIRM's calculation of the worker's social security benefit.

For early retirees, the factor by which benefits are reduced depends on age and service. For example, if the worker retires at age 55 with 20 years of service, the reduction is 50 percent; it would be only 33 percent if the worker had 26 or more years of service. For workers with 30 or more years of service, the reduction drops to zero at retirement ages between 60 and 64.

The pension accrual can vary widely for workers of the same age but with different service and for workers with the same service but of different ages. These accrual differences reflect the fact that many of the features of the benefit and social security formulae involve either age or service or both. Indeed, it is fair to say that the FIRM's benefit formula could hardly be better designed from the perspective of maximizing service and age-related differences in accruals. This variation comes at the cost of a fairly complicated set of provisions which may not be fully understood by individual workers.

Pension Accrual

To describe the effect of the provisions on pension wealth, the accrual profiles for persons born and hired by the FIRM in several different years have been calculated for the calendar period beginning in 1980. For each employee group defined by year of birth and year of hire, accruals are calculated through age 70; the number of years of accruals that are presented thus depends on the age of the employee in 1980. One profile is graphed in figure 5.1. It is used as an illustration to explain the derivation of such profiles. Profiles for different employee and age groups are discussed in the next section.

The graph shows the pension accrual profile for male managers born in 1930 and hired by the FIRM in 1960. By 1980, they were 50

FIGURE 5.1 – Pension wealth accrual, social security accrual and wage earnings for male managers born in 1930 and hired in 1960, in real 1985 dollars.

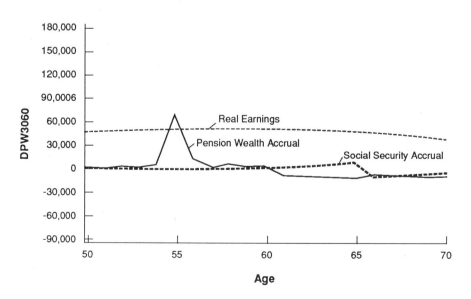

and had 20 years of service with the FIRM. (To calculate pension accrual, we have used the convention that a person hired in a given year has one year of experience in that year. Thus in some of the tables, the person used in this example would be assumed to have 21 years of experience in 1980.) The accrual of social security benefits is shown on the same graph. Predicted wage earnings (see appendix III) for each year are also shown. These predictions are based on actual average earnings of FIRM employees, by age and years of service. All of the numbers presented in this chapter and the next are in real 1985 dollars.

At age 50, in 1980, the typical male manager has wage earnings of about $48,446 per year. Compensation in the form of pension accrual is $2,646, or about 6 percent of wage earnings. If the manager were to retire at this age, he would be entitled to benefits at 65, based on his earnings in the seven or eight preceding years. The benefits would not be available until age 65, and thus have a relatively low present value at age 50.

As described above, normal retirement benefits for a worker retiring before age 55 can be taken earlier, as early as age 55, but they will be reduced actuarially such that the present discounted value of the benefits as of the age of retirement remains unchanged. The reduction in the benefit will be just enough to offset the fact that benefits will be received for more years. If the person remains in the FIRM until age 55 and then retires, however, benefits are available immediately and the reduction in benefits for early retirement is less than the actuarial reduction. In addition, the worker who remains until age 55 and then retires is eligible to receive a supplemental benefit until age 65 equal to his social security offset. Thus there is a very large increase in pension wealth at age 55, $72,527, corresponding to the large spike in the graph. In effect, there is a bonus of $72,527 for remaining in the FIRM from age 54 to 55.

Pension accrual falls after age 55 to about 10 percent of the wage at age 60 (in 1990). Accrual is larger after age 55 than just before age 55 primarily because the early retirement reduction factor, if the worker remains until 55, is less than it would be if he (she) left the FIRM before 55. (If he (she) leaves before 55, the reduction is actuarially fair.) But as the worker ages beyond 56, this effect is partially offset by the fact that an additional year of service adds only 1 percent, instead of 2 percent to benefits. Pension accrual is in fact negative beginning at age 61 (in 1991). Indeed, between ages 61 and 65, the loss in pension benefits is equivalent to about 20 percent of wage compensation.

The loss in compensation between ages 60 and 61 is equivalent to a wage cut of about 14 percent. The worker has 30 years of service at that age and, because of the plan's early retirement reduction factors, is already eligible for full retirement benefits. Thus no increase in benefits will result for working another year, as was the case before 30 years of service. In addition, for each year that benefits are not taken between ages 55 and 65, the receipt of benefits for a year without the social security adjustment (reduction) is foregone. This advantage is lost at age 65 (in 1955). Thereafter, the loss in benefits from working an additional year is smaller because this formerly

FIGURE 5.2 – Pension wealth accrual, social security accrual and wage earnigs for male managers born in 1960 and hired in 1980, in real 1985 dollars.

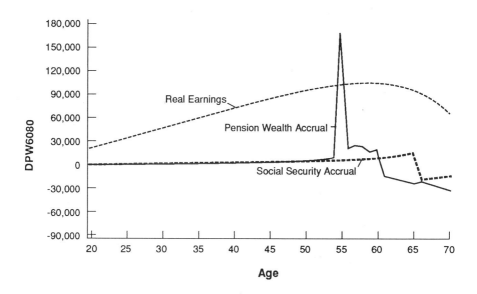

foregone opportunity is no longer available. In addition, the accruals depend on the social security adjustment, and to a small extent on the updating of the years used in the calculation of the earnings base.

Social security accrual for the male manager considered in figure 5.2 ranges from about $1,000 to $8,000 between age 50 and 65. After 65, social security accrual becomes negative, about −$8,500 at age 66.

In summary, the typical manager in the FIRM, making about $48,000 per year in wage earnings at age 60, would lose about $42,000 in pension wealth were he to continue working until age 65. Thus, in addition to the expected concentration of retirement at age 55, we would expect a large proportion of this group to retire before 65. After age 65, social security benefit accrual also becomes negative. At 66, the loss in private pension benefits and social security benefits together amounts to about 32 percent of wage earnings at that age. This suggests a concentration of retirement at 65 as well.

FIGURE 5.3 – Cumulated total income from employment versus year of retirement, male managers born in 1930 and hired in 1960.

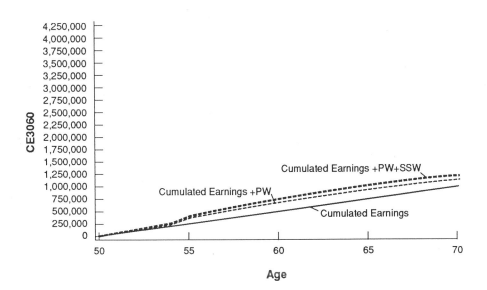

The data in figure 5.1 are shown in the standard budget constraint form in figure 5.3. Total pretax compensation, including wage earnings, social security wealth, and pension wealth, is graphed against age, beginning in 1980. The vertical axis shows the total resources accumulated with interest up to age 65 that the person would acquire from employment with this FIRM. Accumulated earnings before 1980 are ignored in the graph.

There is a discontinuous jump in the graph at age 55. For reasonable preferences for income (that can be used for consumption) versus retirement leisure, one would expect to see a large proportion of workers facing this constraint retiring at age 55 and most retiring prior to age 65. This graph, however, does not suggest the strong concentration of retirement exactly at age 65, that is revealed in the data presented below.

Additional graphs showing pretax wage earnings, pension accrual, and social security accrual over the working span are shown in figures 5.2 and 5.4; again, the first shows accruals by year, and the

FIGURE 5.4 – Cumulated total income from employment versus year of retirement, male managers born in 1960 and hired in 1980.

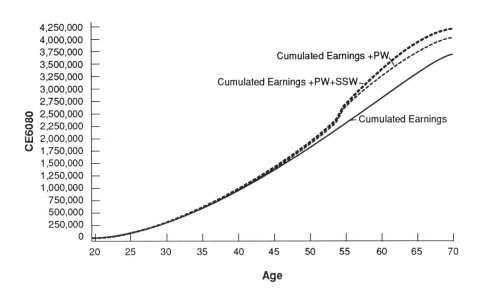

second shows cumulated amounts in the standard budget constraint form. These graphs pertain to a male manager who is hired in 1980, at age 20, and who continues working with the FIRM until age 70. For such workers, the pension accrual at age 55 is $168,000, equivalent to 164 percent of the wage at that age. Wage earnings for this group reach a maximum at age 59. Pension benefit accrual becomes negative at age 61, and social security benefit accrual becomes negative at age 65. In the first year of work after age 65 the loss in pension benefits and social security benefits together amounts to $40,000, about 45 percent of wage earnings at that age. Thus the lifetime budget constraint shows an upward discontinuity at age 55 and a decline in the rate of wage increase around age 60. The decline is especially abrupt after age 65. Retirement at age 55, between 55 and 65, and possibly at 65 would seem to be quite likely for workers facing budget constraints like this one. The calculations underlying the pension accruals, are explained in appendix II.

Variation in Accrual Profiles by Age and Year of Hire

The two accrual profiles discussed above pertain to persons who were born in a given year and who were hired by the FIRM in a given year. The profile in the calendar period beginning in 1980 may be quite different for persons of different ages and with different years of service. Thus, profiles have been calculated for several additional groups, 15 in all, defined by year of birth and year of hire, as follows:

Year of Birth		Year of Hire			
1960	1980				
1950	1980	1975			
1940	1980	1975	1970		
1930	1980	1975	1970	1960	
1920	1980	1975	1970	1960	1950

Pension accruals for managers with these birth and hire years are shown in appendix table 16. Those born in 1940 reach age 55 in

1995, and for each of these groups there is a discontinuous increase in pension wealth in that year. It is \$29,639 for those with 15 years of service in that year and \$82,953 for those with 25 years of service. Comparable jumps occur in 1985 for those born in 1930. Accruals are often negative for persons over 60.

Pension accruals provide a large incentive for some groups to stay in the FIRM for another year and strong incentive for others to leave. For example, staying with the FIRM in 1985 brings pension accrual of \$72,527 for 55-year-old managers with 25 years of service (born in 1930 and hired in 1960), but a loss of \$14,936 for 65-year-olds with 35 years of experience (born in 1920 and hired in 1950). Thus there is enormous variation in the effective compensation for continued service. One might expect therefore that some groups would be much more likely than others to retire in a given year.

In some instances there are erratic fluctuations from one year to the next, from negative to positive to negative for example. This typically occurs if an increase in benefits in one year is not followed by a comparable increase in the next. For example, suppose that the normal retirement benefit is higher in year a than in either year $a-1$ or in year $a+1$. Then the accrual from year $a-1$ to year a will tend to be positive, but the accrual from year a to year $a+1$ will tend to be negative. Dropping a low earnings year and adding a higher one in the calculation of the earnings base may create this effect. Other provisions in the pension calculation formula may do so as well. For convenience, total cumulated pension wealth is shown in appendix table 17 for the same groups. Social security accruals and cumulated social security wealth are shown in appendix tables 18 and 19 respectively. Pretax annual wage earnings and cumulated pretax earnings are shown in appendix tables 20 and 21.

Graphs of two of the profiles are shown in figures 5.3 and 5.4; several others are shown below. Young new hires will have rapid wage growth in the subsequent 20 years, but very little accrual of pension wealth. This is shown in figure 5.2 above for persons born in 1960, and 20 years old at the time of hire in 1980. Their incomes will rise from about \$20,000 in 1980 to over \$70,000 in the year

2000, when they are 40 years old. But even in 2000 their pension accrual will be only $1,558. Their total accrued pension wealth at age 40 will be only $11,894, a very small fraction (1.2 percent) of their total earnings over the period.

A manager hired in 1980, but born in 1940, will have much lower wage growth over the next 20 years, from about $28,000 in 1980 to under $52,000 at age 60 in 2000. This person will also have little pension wealth accrual through age 54, when his total pension wealth will be less than $13,000. In 1995, however, when the person is 55 and eligible for early retirement, it will increase by almost $30,000 to a total of over $47,000. In the next few years, accrual is less than $7,000 per year. The age 55 spike in accrual suggests a potential concentration of retirement among this group at age 55 (in 1995). But the actual pension that would be received is still very small, only about 12 percent of salary (from tables not shown). Thus retirement may be unlikely.

Managers of the same age, but hired 10 years earlier, may be much more likely to retire in that year. They experience a much sharper increase in pension wealth in 1985, from just under $42,000 to over $133,000. The pension benefit to wage replacement rate at 55 for this group is about 26 percent. But accrual after 55 remains positive for this group; pension wealth increases to almost $209,000 by age 60. Thus pension wealth accrual may still provide a substantial incentive to remain with the FIRM.

In contrast, persons born in 1920 and hired by the FIRM at age 40 (in 1960) will have essentially no pension accrual in 1985, and, indeed, it will become negative in a few years. Earnings for this group are declining as well. One might think that persons who are in this group and are still working would be likely to retire. But, if still working, they chose not to retire earlier, when compensation from continued work began to decline. They would have been eligible for early retirement at age 55 (in 1975), when they had been employed for 15 years.

At that time they would have faced earnings and pension accrual profiles like those born and hired 10 years later (in 1930 and 1970 respectively) and who thus had 15 years of service at age 55 (in

1985), when pension accrual was at a maximum. Thereafter, accrual declines and becomes negative around age 65, after 25 years of service. That the group born in 1920 and hired at age 40 didn't retire earlier may suggest that their preferences are such that they are also not likely to retire in a given subsequent year either. They may want to work more than others and that's why they didn't retire when pension accrual and earnings started to decline. In addition, however, the group had not accumulated substantial pension wealth at any time, even before it began to decline, and thus may always have been in a poor position to leave the labor force.

Variation by Employee Type

The pension accrual profiles for other employee groups look very much like those described above. Accrual is minimal during the first years of service. There is typically a discontinuous increase in pension wealth at age 55. And accrual typically becomes negative after 30 years of service, sometimes before that. Social security accrual

FIGURE 5.5 – Pension wealth accrual, social security accrual and wage earnings for salesmen born in 1960 and hired in 1980, in real 1985 dollars.

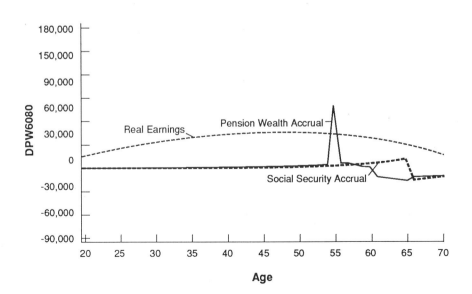

FIGURE 5.6 – Cumulated total income from employment versus year of retirement, salesmen born in 1960 and hired in 1980.

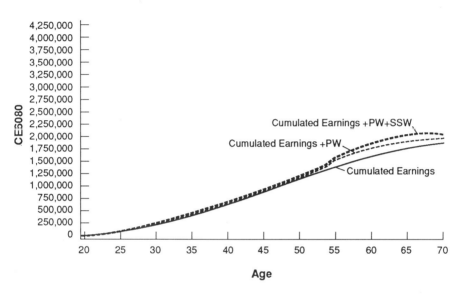

becomes negative after 65. The major differences among the groups stem from different age-earnings profiles. An illustration of the similarity and difference is provided by graphs like that in figures 5.2 and 5.4, but for a different employee group. They are shown in figures 5.5 and 5.6 for salesmen. The data, like those graphed in figure 5.2, pertain to persons born in 1960 and hired in 1980. Thus they pertain to compensation over the lifecycle for persons who remain in the FIRM. As is clear from the graphs, the accrual profiles are qualitatively similar; but there are some important differences.

First, managers earn more than the other employee groups. The wage earnings profiles also differ in shape. The peak earnings for managers occur at age 59. At age 66, if they still are in the labor force, 45 percent of their wage earnings are offset by negative pension and social security accrual. The earnings of salesmen peak much earlier, at age 50. At age 66, almost 95 percent of their wage earnings are offset by loss in pension and social security wealth. Thus this effect creates a greater incentive for the salesmen than for the managers to retire after age 65.[8] The peak wage earnings for saleswomen occurs at age 57; at 66 almost 75 percent of their wage earnings are offset by pension and social security wealth losses. The peak earnings for male and female office workers occurs at ages 59 and 62, respectively. At age 66, 48 and 46 percent, respectively, of their earnings would be offset by loss in pension and social security wealth.[9]

Summary

Pension accrual in the FIRM, a large Fortune 500 company, exhibits a dramatic increase at the FIRM's early retirement age with accrual beyond that age typically small or negative depending on the worker's age and service. The early retirement accrual spike reflects the FIRM's less than actuarial reduction in early retirement benefits as well as its payment to early retirees of a supplemental benefit between the age of retirement and age 65. Workers in the FIRM have a significant incentive to remain with the FIRM until early retirement and then face a possibly significant incentive to leave the FIRM. The retirement incentive generated by the FIRM's pension plan is quite substantial when compared to that generated by social security.

Consideration of the FIRM's accrual profiles together with those discussed in chapters 3 and 4 suggests that ERISA legislation has not precluded significant backloading within U.S. pension plans. Rather than backload pension benefits by requiring a very long period of service prior to vesting, pension plans can effectively backload benefits by requiring very long periods of service prior to the receipt of significant benefits. Workers with more than 10 years of service (5 years under the 1986 Tax Reform Act) who are terminated in highly backloaded plans prior to the age of early retirement will receive a benefit, but the benefit may be quite small. In its effect, the current system permits essentially the same behavior of terminating a worker prior to a specific age and, therefore, depriving the worker of his (her) benefits that occurred prior to ERISA when firms were free to set freely service requirements for vesting.

6

The Relationship Between Retirement, Age, and Years of Service

This chapter examines the relationship of retirement to age and years of service. Its objective is to consider the extent to which retirement behavior accords with the budget constraints described in chapter 5. To do this, we consider empirical hazard rates by age and years of service.

Empirical Hazard Rates

Hazard rates by age and years of service are shown for all employees combined in table 6.1. The yearly hazard rate is the proportion of those employed at the beginning of the year who retire—more strictly speaking, leave the firm—during the forthcoming year. Several aspects of the data stand out. There is substantial turnover in the first nine years of employment, especially during the first five years. On average, about 15 percent of those employed five years or less leave in a given year. The table shows rates only for employees 40 and older. The departure rates are somewhat higher for younger workers, 16 or 17 percent for those employed five years or less and 10 to 12 percent for those employed six to nine years. There is a sharp decline in departure rates at 10 years of service, when employees are about to become vested in the pension plan. Before the early retirement age, 55, the typical decline is from 8 or 9 to 4 or 5 percent. After 55, when vesting carries with it eligibility for early retirement, it is much sharper, often from 10 percent or more to 3 percent or less.

The availability of early retirement benefits at 55 apparently has a substantial effect on retirement. Before 55 departure rates are typically around 2 percent. At 55, they jump to 10 percent or more. It is important to notice that the departure rates stay at that level until

Table 6.1
Empirical Hazard Rates, by Age and Years of Service,
All Employee Groups (percent)

						Years of Service								
Age	5	6–9	10	11–15	16–20	21–23	24	25	26	27	28	29	30	31+
40	15	8	5	7	4	3	0							
41	14	9	5	7	5	5	3	5						
42	14	10	8	8	4	2	2	2	0	0				
43	15	7	6	5	4	4	4	3	2	0	0	0		
44	13	8	5	7	3	2	3	1	1	1	0	0	0	
45	11	7	5	6	6	4	3	1	4	2	3	5	0	5
46	12	9	3	5	3	4	4	1	0	5	2	2	0	0
47	14	8	8	5	4	3	3	4	4	4	0	4	2	0
48	12	7	5	6	4	4	2	5	1	2	4	2	3	2
49	14	9	4	7	4	3	5	1	1	1	1	2	0	0
50	14	8	4	6	4	3	3	2	2	1	1	3	2	3
51	14	9	3	5	3	3	5	2	3	4	2	2	2	5
52	11	7	5	6	4	4	2	4	2	4	1	3	6	6
53	12	7	4	7	4	3	3	3	3	2	3	3	3	3
54	11	7	4	6	4	2	4	2	2	3	1	0	1	3
55	9	5	4	11	9	11	13	10	13	11	12	7	9	9
56	11	6	6	12	11	12	7	8	11	11	12	16	14	12
57	12	10	1	11	8	9	10	8	9	9	3	14	11	11
58	13	10	2	8	8	12	13	11	13	15	9	10	13	12
59	7	10	2	17	8	11	17	14	13	14	9	10	12	15
60	9	9	3	15	12	19	16	17	20	16	20	15	19	26
61	9	7	2	16	17	15	19	12	25	16	23	21	24	30
62	11	15	7	27	34	37	34	33	38	40	42	34	30	41
63	14	18	4	33	35	37	43	35	43	41	62	33	47	40
64	5	8	3	36	33	34	18	32	26	27	42	53	41	34
65	12	35	45	57	52	54	44	55	57	70	50	54	69	59
66	26	17	25	16	16	43	50	16	20	25	38	33	9	24
67	13	28	18	32	17	29	0	14	21	0	13	33	50	21
68	13	50	50	15	25	11	0	50	0	29	0	0	0	12

age 60, when there is another jump in the rate of departure. The jump at 60 corresponds to the age at which pension accrual becomes negative for many employees. (For those with 25 or more years of service, benefits increase at y instead of x percent per year. After age 60, with 30 years of service, there is no early retirement reduction; full retirement benefits are available.)

To understand the potential importance of the early retirement benefits, suppose that if it were not for this inducement, the departure rates would remain at 3 percent until age 60, instead of the 10 or 12 percent rates that are observed. (Notice that the departure rates for employees aged 55 to 61 who are in their 10th year of service—not yet vested and hence not eligible for early retirement benefits—are also 2 or 3 percent on average.) Departure at 3 percent per year would mean that 14 percent of those who were employed at 55 would have left before age 60. At a departure rate of 11 percent per year, 44 percent would leave between 55 and 59. Such a difference, even if only for a small proportion of all firms, can have a very substantial effect on aggregate labor force participation rates, even after one accounts for those workers who leave their main jobs and become reemployed. It is in part the dramatic fall in labor force participation rates for the older population that has motivated research such as ours.

The jump in departure rates at 60, especially noticeable for persons with 25 or more years of service, has been mentioned just above. There is another sharp increase in departure rates at 62 when social security benefits are first available. (There is no sharp kink in the budget constraint at this age because of the actuarially fair increase in social security benefits if their receipt is postponed until age 65.) The increase at 62 is also noticeable for employees with less than 10 years of service and not yet vested in the firm's pension plan. They can take social security benefits, of course.

Finally, there is a very sharp increase in the departure rate at age 65. At this age the loss in social security benefits with continued work induces a kink in the budget constraint. As described above, the budget constraint for many workers becomes essentially flat at this age, due to negative pension accruals and falling wage earnings, as well as the loss in social security wealth. The fall in wage earnings and pension wealth typically begins at an earlier age, as emphasized above. It is important to keep in mind that the large departure rates before 65 mean that most employees have left well before that age. Thus high departure rates at 65 indicate only that a large proportion of the few that continue work until 65 retire then. The cumulative hazard rates below highlight this point.

A more compact version of table 6.1 is shown in table 6.2 for salesmen. About 40.7 percent of employees are salesmen and saleswomen, about 56.2 percent are office workers, and only 3.1 percent managers. Thus for purposes of comparison, it is best to have in mind the accrual and budget constraint graphs for sales and office workers. These results confirm the findings for all employees discussed above. They may be summarized briefly:

- There is a large increase in the departure rates at the early retirement age of 55, but only for vested employees, those with at least 10 years of service. For employees with 16 or more years of service, the jump in departure rates increases noticeably with age.
- The departure rates remain at these higher rates through age 59.
- At age 60, the departure rates increase precipitously for persons with 30 or more years service for whom full benefits are available; there is no longer an early retirement reduction and subsequent pension accrual is negative.
- When social security benefits become available at 62, the departure rates increase very sharply, but apparently only for those who are vested in the FIRM plan, contrary to the results for all employees taken together.
- Finally, there is a large increase in departure rates at 65, after which social security accrual becomes strongly negative.

Cumulative hazard rates for all employees are shown in table 6.3 for three years, together with the rates by age. The cumulative rates are one minus the percent who have departed. These departure rates were obtained by calculating hazard rates over the next four years separately for persons who were age 50 in 1980, age 51 in

Table 6.2
Empirical Hazard Rates for Salesmen by Age
and Years of Service

Age	<10	11–15	16–20	21–25	26–30	31–35	36+
			Years of Service				
<50	19	9	5	4	3	--	--
50–54	14	7	4	3	3	2	0
55	11	14	9	11	12	15	--
56–59	14	13	9	11	11	14	--
60	11	12	14	19	14	29	35
61	13	12	13	13	19	32	28
62	12	27	32	38	36	52	35
63	20	28	33	36	47	48	56
64	0	37	36	30	36	38	28
65	34	56	51	50	49	47	43
66	17	28	10	34	18	16	12
67	20	16	25	21	8	5	18

1980, . . . , and age 63 in 1980. Those who were age 50 in 1980 were 51 in 1981, 52 in 1982, etc. Thus these calculations yield hazard rates in different years for employees of the same age. In particular, given employment at age 50, the cumulative rates show the percent still employed at older ages. (The cumulative rates for those aged 50 are all based on the 1980 departure rate of .031. The rates for those aged 51 are all based on the 1981 rate of .033. The 1983 rate for those aged 52 is based on the 1982 rate. The rate for those who were 65 in 1981 is based on the 1983 rate.)

Table 6.3
Cumulative and Yearly Hazard Rates by Calendar Year,
Years of Service, and Age

| Age | Yearly Hazards | | | | Cumulative Hazards | | |
| | 8–10 YOS | 11+ YOS | | | 11+ YOS | | |
	1980	1981	1982	1983	1981	1982	1983
50	7				97	97	97
51	9	3			94	94	94
52	3	5	5		89	89	89
53	0	4	4		85	86	86
54	4	3	4	2	83	83	84
55	5	11	12	10	74	73	75
56	4	12	14	10	66	63	68
57	2	9	12	11	60	56	61
58	5	10	14	12	54	48	54
59	2	11	20	10	48	38	48
60	4	17	29	17	40	27	40
61	0	17	32	18	33	18	33
62	8	36	48	31	21	10	23
63	14	37	54	37	13	5	14
64		29	49	26	10	2	11
65			58	45	5	1	6
66							

Note first that departure rates of employees who have been in the firm for only 8 to 10 years and are not yet vested are very low at every age, as emphasized above. And again, the increase in the departure rates at 55, 60, 62, and 65 stands out. Based on the 1981 and 1982 departure rates, only 48 percent of those employed at 50 would still be employed at 60, and then 17 percent of these would leave. Only 10 percent would remain until age 65 and then about 50 percent of these would leave.

The data also show the effect of a special early retirement incentive that was in effect in 1982 only. The incentive program provided a bonus to employees who were eligible for early retirement in 1982; that is, those who were vested and were 55 years old or older. The bonus was equivalent to three months salary for 55-year-old employees and increased to 12 months salary for 60-year-olds. At age 65, the bonus was 12 months salary for employees with 20 or fewer years of service and declined to 6 months salary for those with 30 to 39 years of service.

It is clear that the effect of the incentive was large. The departure rates for 1981 and for 1983 are virtually identical. But the rates were much higher in 1982. For example, the departure rate for 60-year-olds was 17 percent in 1981 and in 1983, but 32 percent in 1982. For those age 63, the departure rate was 37 percent in 1981 and in 1983, but 54 percent in 1982. Of those employed at age 50, 40 percent would still have been employed after age 60 based on the 1981 and 1983 departure rates. Only 27 percent would remain after age 60 based on the 1982 rates.[10]

Even under the normal plan, only 10 percent of those employed at age 50 would still be employed at 65. Only 1 percent would remain until 65 with the special incentive.

Summary

Favorable early retirement benefits have a very strong effect on departures from the FIRM, possibly increasing departure rates between ages 55 and 60 by as much as 30 percentage points (e.g., from 14 to 44 percent).

The loss in compensation due to negative pension accrual for many employees after age 60 and negative social security accrual after age 65 apparently also induce departure; only 58 percent of those employed at age 54 remain through 64. About half of the few remaining at 65 retire at that age.

The special early retirement incentive offered by the FIRM in one year increased departure rates very substantially.

7
Summary and Conclusions

This monograph begins with an examination of pension accrual for a representative sample of U.S. defined benefit plans. While the present value of pension accrual is typically a small component of total labor compensation, at many ages and years of service pension accrual significantly raises total compensation, and at other age and service combinations, (negative) pension accrual significantly lowers total compensation. For a sizeable fraction of defined benefit plans, the special shape of age- and service-pension accrual profiles produce significant incentives to remain with one's current employer prior to at least early retirement. After the age of normal retirement, and, often, early retirement, pension accrual profiles typically provide substantial incentives to leave employment. These retirement incentives appear large when compared, for example, with the retirement incentives arising under social security. Hence, the structure of private pensions may have contributed substantially to the recent large reduction in the labor force participation in the United States.

The monograph also examines in considerable detail the provisions of the pension plan in a large corporation. The implications of the provisions are again described by pension accrual profiles. The pension accrual profiles are set forth together with standard age-earnings profiles and social security accrual profiles in the form of lifetime budget constraints. The plan provides strong incentives to retire beginning at age 55. After age 65, negative pension accruals and negative social security accruals effectively impose almost a 100 percent tax rate on wage earnings for many employees of the FIRM.

Departure rates from the FIRM have been compared with economic incentives inherent in the plan provisions. It is clear from this descriptive analysis that the inducements in the plan provisions to retire early have had a very substantial effect on departure rates from the FIRM. Indeed over 50 percent of those employed by the FIRM at age 50 leave before 60, and 90 percent leave before age 65. The jumps in departure rates at specific ages coincide precisely with the discontinuities and kink points in the worker compensation profiles that result from the pension plan provisions together with wage earnings profiles and social security accrual.

A great deal of effort has been devoted to estimating the effect of social security provisions on labor force participation. In particular, Hausman and Wise (1985), Burtless (1986), and Hurd and Boskin (1984) have attempted to estimate the effect on labor force participation of the increases in social security benefits during the early 1970s. It would appear from the results here that the effects of these across-the-board increases in social security benefits are likely to be small relative to the effects of the private pension provisions. For example, it seems clear that shifting the age of early retirement from 55 to say 60 would have a very dramatic effect on departure rates from the FIRM. Leaving the early retirement age at 55, but eliminating negative pension and social security accruals would apparently also have a substantial effect on retirement rates.

The shape of pension accrual profiles appears to rule out the spot market theory of labor market equilibrium. Under the alternative, contractual view of labor markets, pension accrual profiles can be understood as mechanisms to limit worker mobility and to provide carrot- and stick-type incentives to continue working diligently.

This presumes that pension accrual profiles are well understood by both employers and workers. In our view, the great complexity of pension provisions makes it quite difficult for either employers or workers, in the absence of assistance from actuaries, to calculate correctly their accrued pension benefits. While a few firms, including the large FIRM examined here, provide accrual information annually to their workers, most, apparently, do not. It also appears that many firms with access to actuaries do not have their actuaries calculate worker-specific accrual for their own internal use.

The backloading of pension accrual in the presence of limited worker and employer understanding of such backloading raises a variety of quite important questions. Do workers over- or under-value their accrued vested pension benefits? Do workers over- or undersave because they under- or over-value their pensions? Are workers who leave highly backloaded firms prior to the age of early retirement, at which age accrual is often very substantial, aware of the often substantial pension costs of their actions? Is accrual backloading raising the economic costs of early disability, because workers who become disabled prior to the age of early retirement receive less generous pensions then those who remain through early retirement? These and related questions need to be asked by employers, workers, and, apparently, by the United States Congress.

NOTES

1. This assumes no other explicit or implicit fringe benefits.

2. Bulow (1979) appears to be the first discussion of these discontinuities. Lazear (1981; 1983) presents empirical analysis of this issue.

3. In particular, if the percent decrease in the wage, $[W(a+1)-W(a)]/W(a+1)$, is less than the percentage increase in years of employment, $1/t$, benefits would decrease.

4. This example, and subsequent ones as well, assume that the benefit depends on average earnings over the last five years of service, rather than the last year alone.

5. We make no use here of the truncated earnings data contained in the RHS social security earnings records.

6. The 1,183 earnings-based plans with ten-year cliff vesting account for 51 percent of plans weighted by pension coverage.

7. Our calculations ignore service requirements for early retirement, since this inclusion could have considerably complicated our accrual computations. Excluding early retirement service requirements from the analysis is not likely to significantly alter the results. Virtually all workers covered by such requirements are enrolled in plans with early retirement service requirements of 15 years or less (Kotlikoff and Smith 1983).

8. Managerial compensation is primarily in the form of salary, whereas the compensation of salesmen is in the form of commissions to a large extent. They may be more like self-employed or piece rate workers. In particular, their earnings may be determined to a large extent by the number of hours that they choose to work. This may also affect the relationship between compensation and retirement. FIRM officials inform us, however, that most salespeople work only for the FIRM. To the extent that the numbers of hours that they work do not decline substantially with the wage, profiles reflect age-productivity profiles.

9. There should be no presumption that men and women classified by us as office workers are performing the same jobs. The classification does not assure that.

10. This comparison may not be precise because the special incentive, were it to be prolonged, would alter the retirement rates prior to each of the ages considered in 1982.

Appendix I
Pension Accrual Formulae with Early Retirement

The source of discontinuities in age-accrual profiles is clarified by considering a simple earnings-related defined benefit plan with cliff vesting at 10 years of service. Vested accrued benefits are clearly zero prior to the age at which the worker has 10 years of credited service in the plan. Let $R(a,t)$ denote the ratio of $I(a)$ to $W(a)$ for a worker age a with t years of tenure. Then $R(a,t)$ is zero for $t < 9$. If a person age a with 9 years of service works an additional year, the ratio of the increment to the wage $W(a)$ is:

$$(A1) \quad R(a, 9) = \frac{B(a,t)A(55)(1+d)^{-10}(1+r)^{-[55-(a+1)]}}{W(a)}.$$

In (A1), $B(a,t)$ is the retirement benefit available to the worker who terminates employment with the plan sponsor at age a after t years of service, but who delays receipt of pension benefits until the plan's normal retirement age. The normal and early retirement ages assumed for this stylized plan are 65 and 55 respectively. Terminating workers are, however, eligible for early retirement benefits. Our hypothetical plan reduces benefits by d percent for each year that early retirement precedes normal retirement. The benefit reduction rate, d, could be greater than, equal to, or less than the actuarial fair rate. Today most plans offering early retirement appear to stipulate less than actuarially fair reduction rates; consequently, the formulae presented here assume that workers always gain by receiving their vested accrued benefits at the earliest possible date.

The function $A(55)$ is the actuarial discount factor that transforms benefit flows initiating at age 55 into expected stocks of pension wealth at age 55. Expectations here are taken with respect to longevity. Thus $A(55)$ is the annuity value of a dollar's worth of pension benefits to be received each year until death, beginning at age 55. For simplicity assume that the probability of dying prior to age 55 is zero. Hence, the present value at age a of $A(55)$ is $A(a) = A(55) (1+r)^{-(55-a)}$ for $a \leq 55$. If pension benefits are determined as a constant λ times the product of final year's earnings and service, and there is no offset for receipt of social security benefits, $B(a,t)$ is simply:

$$(A2) \quad B(a,t) = \lambda W(a)t,$$

and

$$(A3) \quad R(a,9) = \lambda(1+d)^{-10}(1+r)^{-[55-(1+1)]}A(55)10 \cdot \frac{W(a+1)}{W(a)}.$$

R(a,t), for t increasing pari-passus with age, is zero prior to t equals 9 and jumps at t equals 9 to the value given in (A3). Cliff vesting thus produces spikes in the accrual profile such as that in figure 2.2 at 10 years of service. Between the age at cliff vesting and age 55, pension wealth Pw(a) is given by:

$$(A4) \quad Pw(a) = \lambda W(a)(1+d)^{-10}(1+r)^{-(55-a)}A(55)t,$$

and the increment to pension wealth I(a) divided by the wage W(a) is given by

$$(A5) \quad R(a,t) = \lambda(1+d)^{-10}(1+r)^{-[55-(a+1)]}A(55)t \left| \frac{W(a+1)}{W(a)} \frac{t+1}{t} - 1 \right|.$$

Equations (A5) and (A3) suggest a drop in R(a,t) as a increases to a + 1 concurrent with an increase in t from 9 to 10. Equation (A5) will be positive if the term in brackets exceeds zero. This will be the case if the percent increase in the wage plus the percent increase in years employed (1/t) is greater than zero. Assuming the term in brackets is positive and is roughly constant, R(a,t) will increase exponentially due to the exponential decline in the discount factor, $(1+r)^{-[55-(a+1)]}$, as a approaches 55.

If the value of d is considerably less than actuarially fair, a discontinuity in R(a,t) occurs at the early retirement age, 55. At ages 55 and 56 we have:

$$(A6) \quad Pw(55) = \lambda W(55)(1+d)^{-10}A(55)t,$$

and

$$(A7) \quad Pw(56) = \lambda W(56)(1+d)^{-9}A(56)(t+1).$$

Hence,

$$(A8) \quad R(55,t) = \lambda(1+d)^{-10}(1+r)A(55)t \left[\frac{W(56)}{W(55)} \left(\frac{t+1}{t} \right) \frac{A(56)}{A(55)} \frac{(1+d)}{(1+r)} - 1 \right].$$

Assuming wage growth at 54 is close to that at 55 and A(56) approximately equals A(55), then R(55,t) primarily differs from R(54,t−1) because the first terms in the bracket in (A5) is now multiplied by (1+d) while the second term, −1, is multiplied by (1+r). Since r exceeds d by assumption, R(55,t) can easily be less than R(54,t−1). Indeed, this change in the functional form of R(a,t) can produce sharp drops in accrual rates at the early retirement age for a host of pension plans and a range of realistic economic assumptions. Figure 2.2 illustrates such discontinuities.

It is important to realize that the early retirement reduction, lower wages, and one less year of tenure yield lower benefits at 55 than at 56. The early retirement reduction reduces benefits at the rate d. But if benefits were taken at 55 they could accrue interest at the rate r. Thus by foregoing the early retirement option of receiving benefits at 55, a cost is incurred that depends on the difference r − d. If this loss is not offset by the increase due to wage growth and one year of additional tenure, there will be a drop in the benefit accrual rate between 55 and 56.

The same considerations pertain to benefit increments between 56 and 65. Recall that we have assumed a less than fair early retirement reduction so that benefits accrued before 55 are valued assuming receipt of benefits at the age that yields maximum pension wealth. The optimum time to receive benefits accrued between 55 and 56 is 56, between 56 and 57 it is 57, and so forth. But to gain benefits from working another year, it is necessary to forego the option of immediately taking accrued benefits at an advantageous reduction rate.

Between ages 56 and 65, R(a,t) equals:

$$(A9) \quad R(a,t) = \lambda(1+d)^{-(65-a)} (1+r)A(a)t$$
$$\cdot \left[\frac{W(a+1)}{W(a)} \frac{(t+1)}{t} \frac{A(a+1)}{(a)} \frac{(1+d)}{(1+r)} - 1 \right].$$

In contrast to the R(a,t) formula in (A5) applying to the period between cliff vesting and early retirement, (A9) indicates that the actuarial reduction factor—rather than the interest rate r—imparts an upward tilt in the R(a,t) profile between early and normal retirement, as long as the term in brackets is positive. In (A9) as in (A5) and (A8) the accrual rate, R(a,t) is an increasing function of the rate of nominal wage growth. Larger nominal interest rates reduce accrual rates at all ages, with a negative interaction with age prior to early retirement.

Finally, while equation (9) is unlikely to be negative, wide differences between wage growth and the interest rate r can yield negative increments in pension wealth after the early retirement age. To a first approximation, the bracketed term in equation (9) will be positive if $\Delta W/W + 1/t > r - d$ where $\Delta W/W$ is the percent increase in wages, and $1/t$ is the percent increase in tenure. It is easy to see, however, that low wage growth and high interest rates will yield negative increments. Thus actuarial increments after the early retirement age are very sensitive to assumed rates of wage growth and interest.

Appendix II
Decomposition of Pension Accrual

The calculations underlying the pension accrual in figures 5.1–5.6 are explained in this section. The wage earnings and other dollar values in this section are in current dollars, however, while the graphs are in constant 1985 dollars. The nominal interest rate assumed throughout this analysis is 0.09, and the real interest is assumed to equal 0.03.

The calculations are shown in appendix table 22 for male managers who were born in 1930 and hired by the firm in 1960, the same group whose accrual profile is illustrated in figure 5.1. Columns (1) through (4) are self-explanatory. Column (5) is the average earnings base used to calculate pension benefits. The normal retirement benefit is shown in column (6). It is calculated using the formula in equation 10 above. The social security benefit in column (7) is calculated by the FIRM based on earnings projected forward to age 65. Column (8) is the social security adjustment. Column (9) is (7) minus (8). Column (10) is 1 minus the early retirement adjustment, the proportion of the benefit that remains after the adjustment. Once the person has worked for 30 years there is, according to the FIRM's early retirement reduction provisions, no reduction even though the person is only 60 years old at that time.

The numbers in column (11) equal the numbers in column (10) multiplied by those in column (6). It is the benefit that a person who retired early would receive between the early retirement age and age 65. After age 65, benefits are based on the adjusted retirement benefits, reduced by the early retirement reduction factor. These benefits are shown in column (12), which is (10) times (9).

The annuity value of a dollar received each year from 65 until death is shown in column (13) of appendix table 22. It accounts for the probability that a person will be alive at each year in the future. The probability that a person will live from the current age until 65 is shown in column (14). The current value of a dollar that will be received at age 65 is shown in column (15). At the current age, the present value of the pension benefits that the manager can receive at age 65 is shown in column (16) and is given by (12) × (13) × (14) × (15).

If the manager retires at age 55 or later, he will receive benefits until age 65 that are not reduced by the social security adjustment. He receives the normal retirement benefits in column (6) reduced only by the early retirement reduction factor, (10), and shown in column (11). The present value of these benefits from the year of first collection until age 65 is shown in column (17). These benefits plus those that will be received after age 65, are the present value of his pension wealth and are shown in column (18) ((16) plus (17)).

The change in pension wealth from one year to the next, the pension accrual, is shown in column (19). Recall that accrual at age a, I(a), is given by

(10) $I(a) = Pw(a+1) - Pw(a)(1+r)$

where a is pension wealth and r is the nominal interest rate, taken to be 0.09. Again, these pension accruals, together with social security accruals and the wage, are graphed in figures 5.1, 5.2, and 5.5, but in 1985 dollars. The accrual as a percent of wage earnings is shown in column (20).

Appendix III
Earnings Model

Estimating Age-Earnings Profiles

Earnings histories from 1969 are available for workers employed during the period 1980 through 1984. To explain the main features of the estimation procedure, appendix figure 1 describes the earnings of two persons who are in the data set for seven years. The first person is age 40 to 46 over these seven years, and the second is age 45 to 51. (They could also have different years of service, but that is ignored in this example.) Earnings by age for the typical person in the FIRM are represented by the solid line in the middle of the graph. The first person has higher earnings than the average employee. His earnings exceed those of the typical person by an amount u_1, the individual-specific earnings effect for person 1. It may arise, for example, because this person works harder than the typical employee or because he has greater ability or more training. Earnings for person 1 fluctuate from year to year, however. The deviations with age from the central tendency of his earnings, indicated by the person 1 average, are

FIGURE A.1 – Illustration of individual-specific earnings effects

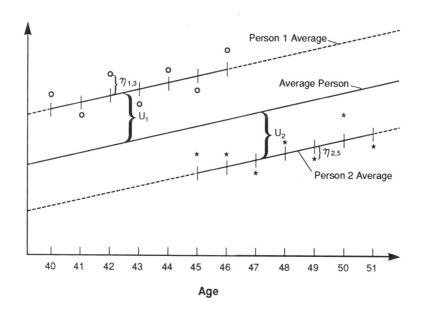

indicated by n_{1t}, where t indicates the deviation in year t. Future earnings for person 1 must be estimated for our analysis. They are indicated by the dashed part of the line. They depend on u_1 and on the estimated relationship between age and earnings, which, aside from the individual-specific term, is assumed to be the same for individuals within a sex-occupation group.

The implications of the estimates are shown for male managers in appendix figure 2. It shows earnings profiles for managers by age of hire in 1980, where the nine profiles on the graph pertain to persons hired at successively older ages—from 20 to 60 in five-year intervals. Earnings are calculated through age 70 for each cohort. First, it is clear that, for any age, earnings increase substantially with years of service. Earnings at the time of hire increase with age, but the bulk of the difference in earnings is accounted for by years of service in the FIRM. For example, persons who are 55 and just hired (profile 8) earn much less than those who are 55, but have been working for the FIRM since age 20 (profile 1). Finally, the decline in earnings for older workers is much greater for long-term employees than for those who have been hired recently.

Similar patterns apply to other employee groups, (graphs not shown), but with some significant variations. The earnings of male office workers at

FIGURE A.2 – Age-earnings profiles for persons hired in 1980, by age when hired, male managers.

the time of hire vary greatly by age, increasing and then declining rapidly. The importance of these profiles for our work is that future expected earnings depend in an important way on the age and years of service of an employee, and the employee group.

In our prediction of earnings beyond 1984 we use the 1984 year dummy and add a 1.5 percent real wage growth factor; i.e., the predicted earnings for year t is the predicted earnings for 1984 times $(1.5)(t-1984)$.

Earnings Equation Specification

To simplify the presentation, we include only one right-hand variable, age. In practice estimation is based on age and years of service. The exact specification is presented below. An earnings equation that captures the ideas discussed above is:

$$(A10) \quad \ln E_{it} = \beta_0 + \beta_1 A_{it} + \beta_2 A_{it}^2 + \epsilon_{it}$$

$$= \mu_{it} + \epsilon_{it}$$

$$\epsilon_{it} = u_i + \eta_{it}$$

$$\text{Var}(\epsilon_{it}) = \text{Var}(u_i) + \text{Var}(\eta_{it}) = \sigma_\epsilon^2, \ \text{Var}(u_i) = \sigma_u^2, \ \text{Var}(\eta_{it}) = \sigma_\eta^2$$

$$\text{Cov}(u_i,\eta_{it}) = \text{Cov}(\eta_{it},\eta_{it},) = 0$$

$$E \equiv \text{Annual earnings}$$

$$A \equiv \text{Age}$$

$$i \equiv \text{Indexes individuals}$$

$$t \equiv \text{Indexes year (e.g., 1978, \ldots, 1983)}$$

$$u_i \equiv \text{Individual-specific earnings effect}$$

$$E_{it} = e^{\mu_{it}} e^{\epsilon_{it}} = e^{\mu_{it}} e^{u_i} e^{\eta_{it}}$$

$$E(E_{it}|\mu_{it},u_i) = e^{\mu_{it}} e^{u_i} E(e^{\eta_{it}}) \doteq e^{\mu_{it}} e^{u_i} (1 + \frac{\sigma_\eta^2}{2}).$$

The last approximation arises because of the nonlinear relationship between earnings and age; i.e., the expected value of exp $[\eta_{it}]$ is not equal to 1, even though the expected value of η_{it} is 0.

In addition to the parameters β, the variances of u and η are also of interest. The first indicates the systematic earnings variation across individuals due to individual-specific effects. The second is a measure of the extent of nonsystematic variation. The method of estimation used here does not allow for the possibility that the individual-specific terms u may be correlated with age. For example, it may be that persons whose earnings are higher, because of the attributes u, are more likely to continue working at older ages. We did obtain such estimates using a differencing procedure. But for our purposes the procedure has two important shortcomings: First, it means that certain age and service parameters are not identified. Second, it imposes the rate of salary increase by age that existed over the period of the data, because this relationship depends only on changes in earnings over the period of the data. (The method we use allows the effect of age to be determined in part by comparison of the earnings of workers with very different ages.) This increase is apparently low relative to longer term increases, and hence may imply expected future increases with age and service that are too low. We also discovered that individual-specific terms based on the method that we have used are not correlated with firm departure rates.

Estimation Method
Estimation of equation (A10) yields residuals

$$e_{it} = \ln E_{it} - \hat{\beta}_0 - \hat{\beta}_1 A_{it} - \hat{\beta}_2 A_{it}^2 .$$

The estimated variance of e_{it} is given by

$$(A11) \quad \hat{\sigma}_\epsilon^2 = \frac{\sum\limits_{i,t} e_{it}^2}{\sum\limits_{i} n_i - k} ,$$

where n_i is the number of observations for person i and k is the number of parameters (3 in this example). To obtain estimates of additional parameters of interest we need to distinguish persons with more than one observation from those with only 1.

a. Using Persons With $n_i \geq 2$
From the residuals for person i the individual-specific effect for i is calculated by

$$(A12) \quad \hat{u}_i = \frac{\sum\limits_{t} e_{it}}{n_i} .$$

The variances η and u are then given, respectively, by

$$(A13) \quad \hat{\sigma}_\eta^2 = \frac{\sum\limits_{i,t} (e_{it} - \hat{u}_i)^2}{\sum\limits_{i} n_i - k - I}$$

and

(A14) $\mathrm{Var}(u_i) = \mathrm{Var}(e_{it}) - \mathrm{Var}(n_{it})$

where I is the number of persons in the sample (in this instance those with $n_i \geq 2$), and

(A15) $\hat{\eta}_{it} = e_{it} - \hat{u}_i$.

b. For Persons With $n_i = 1$

If a person has only one observation we can't distinguish η_{it} from u_i, since we don't observe any variation around an average. First note that if u and η are normally distributed, and thus ϵ_{it} is also,

$$E(u_i | E_{it}) = E(u_i) + \rho_{u,\epsilon} \frac{\sigma_u}{\sigma_\epsilon} (\epsilon_{it} - E(\epsilon_{it}))$$

$$= 0 + \rho_{u,\epsilon} \frac{\sigma_u}{\sigma_\epsilon} (\epsilon_{it} - 0)$$

$$= \rho_{u,\epsilon} \frac{\sigma_u}{\sigma_\epsilon} ,$$

$$\mathrm{Cov}(u_{ui}, \epsilon_{it}) = E[u_i(u_i + \eta_{it})] = \sigma_u^2 ,$$

$$\rho_{u,\epsilon} = \frac{\mathrm{Cov}(u,\epsilon)}{\sqrt{\mathrm{Var}(u)} \cdot \sqrt{\mathrm{Var}(\epsilon)}} = \frac{\sigma_u^2}{\sigma_u \sqrt{\sigma_u^2 + \sigma_\eta^2}} = \frac{\sigma_u}{\sigma_\epsilon} ,$$

$$\rho_{u,\epsilon} \cdot \frac{\sigma_u}{\sigma_\epsilon^2} = \frac{\sigma_u^2}{\sigma_\epsilon^2} ,$$

where ρ is a correlation coefficient. Thus

$$E(u_i \mid \epsilon_{it}) = \frac{\sigma_u^2}{\sigma_\epsilon^2} \epsilon_{it} = \frac{\sigma_\epsilon^2 - \sigma_\eta^2}{\sigma_\epsilon^2} \cdot \epsilon_{it} .$$

If σ_η^2 were 0 and we observed ϵ_{it}, we would assume it represented entirely an individual-specific effect u_i. If σ_u^2 were 0, we would assume the ϵ_{it} were equal to the random term η_{it}, and that there was no individual effect u_i. Letting e_{it} be the sample analog of ϵ_{it} and using the estimates in (19) and (20) for σ_ϵ^2 and σ_η^2 respectively, u_i for persons with only one observation is estimated by

(A16) $\hat{u}_i = \dfrac{\hat{\sigma}_\epsilon^2 - \hat{\sigma}_\eta^2}{\hat{\sigma}_\epsilon^2} \, e_{it} \, .$

And η_{it}

$$\hat{\eta}_{it} = e_{it} - \hat{u}_i \, .$$

c. Predicted Earnings

For estimation of the likelihood that a person will retire in the next year, we need to use predicted earnings in that year. For future analysis we also need to predict earnings in subsequent years as well. The predictions are given by

(A17) $\hat{E}_{it} = e^{\hat{\mu}_{it}} e^{\hat{u}_i} E(e^{\eta_{it}}) = e^{\hat{\mu}_{it} + \hat{u}_i} (1 + \hat{\sigma}_\eta^2/2)$ for $n_i \geq 2$

$\hat{E}_{it} = e^{\hat{\mu}_{it}} e^{\hat{u}_i} E(e^{\eta_{it}}) = e^{\hat{\mu}_{it} + \hat{\hat{u}}_i} (1 + \hat{\sigma}_\eta^2/2)$ for $n_i = 1$.

For out-of-sample estimates, $\hat{\mu}_{it}$ would be predicted from future age, for example.[1]

d. The Estimated Components of Earnings

To consider how much earnings deviate from what might be predicted for that person, or from what that person himself might predict, it is useful to divide earnings into expected and unexpected components. We do that by defining

(A18) $\ln E_{it} \equiv \hat{\mu}_{it} + \hat{u}_i + \hat{\eta}_{it}$

$\hat{\mu}_{it} + \hat{u} \equiv$ "permanent" or "expected" component

$\hat{\eta}_{it} \equiv$ "transitory" or "unexpected" component.

These definitions do not necessarily correspond to usual definitions of permanent versus transitory income, so the expected versus unexpected terminology may be better. In levels the two components are given by

(A19) $\quad E_{it} \equiv e^{\hat{\mu}_{it} + \hat{u}_i} \cdot e^{\hat{\eta}_{it}}$

$\qquad = e^{\hat{\mu}_{it} + \hat{u}_i} + e^{\hat{\mu}_{it} + \hat{u}_i}(e^{\eta_{it}} - 1)$

$\qquad = \dfrac{\text{permanent}}{\text{component}} + \dfrac{\text{transitory}}{\text{component}}$.

A More Detailed Specification of the Earnings Function

Earnings were predicted using the following variables:

Age
Age Squared
Age Squared × Service
Service
Service Squared
Service Squared × Age
Age × Service
Age Squared × Service Squared
Calendar Year Variables for 1969, . . . ,1979 and 1981, . . . , 1983.

The calendar year variables pick up changes in real earnings over time. Each of the year estimates is relative to the 1980 base. The estimated earnings function parameters are shown in appendix table 23.

NOTE

1. Simulated actual future earnings could be obtained by taking a random draw η_{it} from the estimate distribution of η, $N(0,\hat{\sigma}^2)$, for each future year and using the average value of $e^{\hat{\mu}_{it} + \hat{u}_i} e^{\hat{\eta}_{it}}$. In this case there is no need to use the nonlinearity correction.

Table A.1
Weighted Average Accrual Rates for Percent of Earnings Plans With 10-Year Cliff Vesting, by Early and Normal Retirement Age[a]

Early Ret.	55	55	55	60	60	62	62	65
Normal Ret.	55	60	65	60	65	62	65	65
No. of Plans	152	115	513	78	53	19	8	50
Age								
40	.244	.111	.071	.034	.047	.038	.054	.036
41	.045	.022	.013	.007	.010	.016	.009	.010
42	.051	.026	.016	.008	.011	.017	.010	.011
43	.058	.029	.018	.010	.013	.120	.011	.012
44	.066	.033	.020	.011	.015	.029	.013	.014
45	.075	.036	.023	.013	.017	.036	.013	.016
46	.085	.043	.026	.016	.019	.042	.015	.018
47	.097	.050	.031	.028	.022	.047	.017	.021
48	.110	.057	.035	.039	.025	.054	.019	.024
49	.124	.064	.040	.056	.029	.060	.021	.027
50	.141	.077	.046	.065	.034	.068	.023	.031
51	.159	.072	.052	.084	.040	.077	.026	.033
52	.180	.087	.062	.091	.050	.090	.028	.043
53	.204	.099	.072	.105	.060	.101	.032	.050
54	.231	.113	.083	.117	.068	.114	.035	.055
55	.261	.130	.097	.149	.082	.128	.039	.065
56	-.003	.100	.068	.170	.094	.144	.036	.068
57	-.012	.111	.072	.192	.107	.162	.039	.076
58	-.020	.118	.076	.224	.127	.184	.044	.089
59	-.028	.129	.077	.241	.146	.208	.048	.105
60	-.038	.143	.079	.269	.167	.241	.054	.118
61	-.048	-.090	.068	-.061	.113	.220	.059	.128
62	-.058	-.091	.064	-.091	.115	.248	.066	.145
63	-.067	-.091	.056	-.114	.114	-.130	.017	.163
64	-.076	-.092	.053	-.121	.114	-.136	.012	.186
65	-.085	-.094	.044	-.121	.112	-.144	.006	.211
66	-.292	-.169	-.152	-.138	-.088	-.266	-.081	-.194
67	-.294	-.174	-.162	-.155	-.115	-.263	-.080	-.204
68	-.295	-.179	-.171	-.171	-.142	-.260	-.079	-.213
69	-.296	-.182	-.179	-.184	-.162	-.258	-.078	-.221
70	-.297	-.184	-.186	-.196	-.182	-.255	-.077	-.234

a. Plans with early or normal retirement supplements are excluded.

Table A.2
Dispersion of Accrual Ratios for Table 1 Plans With Age 55
Early Retirement and Age 65 Normal Retirement

	Weighted Average Accrual Ratios	Median Accrual Ratios	Minimum Accrual Ratios	Maximum Accrual Ratios	Lowest 5th Percentile	Largest 5th Percentile
No. of Plans	513	513	513	513	513	513
Age						
40	.071	.021	0	.383	0	.201
41	.013	.012	−.025	.071	0	.036
42	.016	.013	−.025	.080	0	.041
43	.018	.014	−.027	.091	0	.046
44	.020	.016	−.026	.103	0	.052
45	.023	.019	−.029	.116	0	.058
46	.026	.023	−.028	.131	0	.066
47	.031	.028	−.024	.162	0	.076
48	.034	.032	−.020	.167	0	.083
49	.040	.039	−.020	.188	0	.093
50	.046	.046	−.011	.212	0	.106
51	.052	.052	−.020	.240	0	.119
52	.062	.061	−.019	.270	0	.140
53	.072	.072	−.015	.305	0	.157
54	.083	.083	−.015	.344	0	.180
55	.097	.100	−.005	.405	0	.208
56	.068	.075	−.065	.424	0	.165
57	.072	.079	−.063	.363	0	.171
58	.076	.083	−.051	.248	0	.183
59	.077	.083	−.046	.286	−.0006	.190
60	.079	.086	−.064	.345	−.014	.204
61	.068	.074	−.156	.339	−.038	.181
62	.064	.068	−.154	.325	−.050	.190
63	.056	.062	−.192	.310	−.115	.191
64	.053	.060	−.221	.460	−.119	.210
65	.044	.052	−.323	.326	−.148	.205
66	−.152	−.136	−.558	.121	−.203	0
67	−.162	−.159	−.550	.060	−.406	0
68	−.171	−.179	−.541	.043	−.412	0
69	−.179	−.190	−.534	.029	−.414	0
70	−.186	−.197	−.618	.014	−.424	0

Table A.3

Weighted Average Accrual Rates for Percent of Earnings Plans With 10-Year Cliff Vesting and Early Retirement at Age 55, by Normal Retirement Age and Social Security Offset[a]

Normal Ret. Offset No. of Plans	55		62		65	
	W/O Offset 135	W Offset 17	W/O Offset 103	O Offset 84	W/O Offset 254	W Offset 259
Age						
40	.260	.073	.175	.030	.121	.016
41	.049	.005	.034	.010	.022	.004
42	.055	.008	.039	.014	.026	.005
43	.062	.010	.044	.017	.029	.006
44	.071	.013	.049	.020	.033	.007
45	.080	.017	.064	.024	.037	.009
46	.090	.030	.064	.027	.041	.011
47	.102	.039	.074	.034	.078	.013
48	.115	.047	.086	.040	.052	.016
49	.130	.061	.100	.049	.058	.019
50	.147	.074	.112	.066	.065	.025
51	.166	.089	.127	.079	.072	.029
52	.187	.108	.143	.096	.081	.041
53	.211	.127	.165	.112	.091	.051
54	.238	.146	.185	.132	.102	.062
55	.269	.175	.213	.155	.116	.076
56	−.008	.042	.090	.115	.078	.058
57	−.016	.036	.092	.120	.077	.065
58	−.025	.040	.103	.135	.076	.076
59	−.034	.034	.096	.140	.073	.082
60	−.043	.025	.087	.143	.069	.091
61	−.052	−.004	.090	.109	.071	.066
62	−.062	−.012	.087	.110	.061	.068
63	−.071	−.024	−.075	−.066	.047	.066
64	−.081	−.026	−.086	−.069	.040	.067
65	−.090	−.032	−.098	−.074	.025	.066
66	−.309	−.109	−.224	−.154	−.203	−.097
67	−.309	−.132	−.248	−.170	−.212	−.108
68	−.308	−.153	−.270	−.184	−.219	−.119
69	−.307	−.172	−.280	−.196	−.227	−.128
70	−.307	−.191	−.290	−.204	−.233	−.136

a. Plans with early or normal retirement supplements are excluded.

117

Table A.4
Weighted Average Accrual Rates for Percent of Earnings Plans With 10-Year Cliff Vesting and Early Retirement at 55, by Normal Retirement Age and Post-Normal Retirement Provision[a]

Normal Retire.	55			62					65				
Provision	Full Credit, Defer.	No Credit, Defer.	Limited Credit, Defer.	Full Credit, Defer.	No Credit, Defer.	No Credit, Immed. Payout or Actuarial Increase	Limited Credit, Defer.	Limited Credit, Immed. Payout or Actuarial Increase	Full Credit, Defer.	No Credit, Defer.	No Credit, Immed. Payout or Actuarial Increase	Limited Credit, Defer.	Limited Credit, Immed. Payout or Actuarial Increase
No. of Plans	18	5	129	76	7	2	66	35	212	207	63	22	9
Age
40	.186	.009	.252	.104	.120	.243	.105	.087	.077	.057	.082	.063	.023
41	.035	.009	.046	.022	.034	.047	.021	.018	.016	.011	.012	.013	.007
42	.040	.009	.053	.028	.039	.053	.024	.021	.018	.012	.013	.015	.014
43	.045	.008	.060	.032	.044	.060	.028	.024	.021	.014	.015	.017	.016
44	.051	.008	.068	.036	.050	.068	.032	.028	.024	.016	.017	.020	.019
45	.058	.007	.077	.041	.057	.076	.050	.033	.028	.018	.019	.025	.022
46	.072	.007	.087	.045	.064	.086	.045	.038	.031	.019	.022	.029	.028
47	.085	.007	.098	.053	.073	.097	.054	.045	.036	.025	.025	.034	.037
48	.096	.007	.111	.063	.082	.110	.062	.051	.040	.026	.028	.039	.045
49	.110	.026	.125	.076	.093	.124	.072	.060	.046	.029	.031	.045	.052
50	.125	.048	.142	.091	.104	.139	.081	.081	.053	.035	.035	.052	.058
51	.143	.054	.160	.106	.119	.156	.094	.093	.060	.040	.039	.054	.067
52	.166	.060	.181	.123	.133	.176	.109	.109	.072	.048	.044	.066	.076
53	.188	.070	.204	.145	.150	.198	.125	.124	.081	.057	.054	.082	.087
54	.214	.074	.231	.164	.168	.223	.147	.140	.092	.068	.063	.094	.098
55	.244	.084	.261	.191	.190	.250	.170	.161	.105	.081	.077	.112	.116

Table A.4 Continued
Weighted Average Accrual Rates for Percent of Earnings Plans With 10-Year Cliff Vesting and Early Retirement at 55, by Normal Retirement Age and Post-Normal Retirement Provision[a]

Normal Retire.	55			62					65				
Pro-vision	Full Credit, Defer.	No Credit, Defer.	Limited Credit, Defer.	Full Credit, Defer.	No Credit, Defer.	No Credit, Immed. Payout or Actuarial Increase	Limited Credit, Defer.	Limited Credit, Immed. Payout or Actuarial Increase	Full Credit, Defer.	No Credit, Defer.	No Credit, Immed. Payout or Actuarial Increase	Limited Credit, Defer.	Limited Credit, Immed. Payout or Actuarial Increase
No. of Plans	18	5	129	76	7	2	66	35	212	207	63	22	9
Age													
56	.015	-.080	-.007	.119	.137	.091	.058	.094	.071	.051	.062	.097	.112
57	.006	-.077	-.016	.116	.145	.073	.070	.094	.074	.054	.067	.098	.116
58	.008	-.075	-.024	.120	.152	.064	.098	.099	.076	.059	.068	.104	.128
59	-.007	-.073	-.033	.116	.161	.053	.097	.105	.075	.062	.071	.108	.127
60	-.017	-.071	-.042	.110	.169	.042	.093	.106	.074	.063	.082	.109	.122
61	-.039	-.070	-.051	.092	.158	-.079	.090	.073	.061	.057	.090	.071	.071
62	-.048	-.069	-.060	.082	.216	-.091	.094	.066	.053	.056	.088	.067	.063
63	-.058	-.068	-.069	-.064	-.378	0	-.033	-.051	.041	.052	.085	.052	.056
64	-.063	-.079	-.078	-.074	-.357	0	-.037	-.063	.038	.048	.083	.048	.049
65	-.071	-.016	-.087	-.085	-.337	0	-.045	-.074	.027	.041	.080	.041	.037
66	-.113	-.018	-.317	-.166	-.318	0	-.026	0	-.154	-.179	0	-.165	-.112
67	-.115	-.020	-.312	-.208	-.314	0	-.260	0	-.175	-.177	0	-.175	-.148
68	-.196	-.021	-.308	-.247	-.309	0	-.257	0	-.194	-.174	0	-.185	-.179
69	-.236	-.020	-.303	-.268	-.304	0	-.256	0	-.211	-.171	0	-.201	-.207
70	-.272	-.023	-.298	-.290	-.299	0	-.251	0	-.226	-.168	0	-.210	-.230

a. Men only. There were no plans with the provisions corresponding to the two deleted categories under the 55 normal retirement heading.

Table A.5

Weighted Average Accrual Rates for Percent of Earnings and Flat Plans With 10-Year Cliff Vesting and Early or Normal Retirement Supplements, by Early and Normal Retirement Ages[a]

Early Ret.	55	55	55	60	60	62
Normal Ret.	55	60	65	60	65	62
No. of Plans	19	56	22	37	2	19
Age						
40	.199	.136	.082	.078	.068	.056
41	.039	.024	.015	.014	.012	.010
42	.045	.027	.018	.016	.013	.011
43	.052	.030	.021	.018	.015	.013
44	.059	.034	.025	.020	.017	.151
45	.068	.038	.030	.022	.019	.180
46	.077	.043	.036	.023	.022	.020
47	.088	.049	.041	.027	.025	.023
48	.100	.055	.048	.030	.028	.026
49	.114	.062	.056	.035	.032	.030
50	.129	.070	.064	.039	.036	.035
51	.148	.080	.074	.044	.040	.029
52	.167	.090	.087	.050	.046	.033
53	.191	.103	.099	.057	.053	.039
54	.220	.117	.113	.066	.061	.044
55	.389	.498	.484	.075	.069	.060
56	−.019	.071	.016	.086	.080	.064
57	−.078	.071	.019	.099	.092	.161
58	−.048	.071	−.021	.114	.107	.097
59	−.057	.069	−.026	.132	.123	.110
60	−.067	1.079	−.008	.643	.233	.127
61	−.085	−.292	−.049	−.208	.048	.146
62	−.093	−.301	−.056	−.212	.045	.183
63	−.108	−.353	−.067	−.227	.039	−.078
64	−.079	−.079	−.006	−.102	.072	−.086
65	−.086	−.043	.018	−.099	.194	−.094
66	−.124	−.088	−.182	−.100	−.048	−.169
67	−.141	−.116	−.195	−.088	−.064	−.111
68	−.150	−.124	−.191	−.092	−.072	−.112
69	−.151	−.132	−.188	−.097	−.112	−.113
70	−.151	−.141	−.186	−.102	−.120	−.114

a. There are no plans in the 62–65 or in the 65–65 early-normal retirement groups.

Table A.6
Weighted Average Accrual Rates for Flat Rate Plans With
10-Year Cliff Vesting, by Early and Normal Retirement Age[a]

Early Ret. Normal Ret.	55 55	55 60	55 65	60 60	60 65	62 62	62 65	65 65
No. of Plans	3	90	106	10	48	3	17	14
Age								
40	.304	.104	.070	.022	.046	.033	.025	.019
41	.052	.027	.012	.004	.008	.006	.004	.006
42	.059	.031	.013	.004	.009	.007	.005	.006
43	.066	.035	.015	.005	.010	.007	.006	.006
44	.075	.039	.017	.006	.012	.008	.007	.007
45	.084	.044	.019	.006	.013	.009	.007	.007
46	.096	.049	.022	.007	.015	.010	.008	.007
47	.108	.052	.025	.029	.017	.011	.009	.008
48	.123	.058	.029	.053	.019	.013	.011	.009
49	.139	.064	.032	.063	.022	.015	.012	.009
50	.158	.073	.037	.067	.025	.016	.013	.010
51	.180	.093	.042	.079	.028	.018	.015	.011
52	.205	.105	.048	.084	.032	.021	.017	.012
53	.235	.121	.054	.098	.037	.024	.020	.014
54	.269	.138	.062	.110	.042	.027	.022	.015
55	.308	.163	.073	.150	.048	.030	.025	.017
56	-.121	.079	.052	.171	.055	.035	.028	.018
57	-.119	.077	.055	.189	.063	.040	.032	.020
58	-.118	.095	.058	.228	.073	.045	.037	.030
59	-.117	.105	.060	.258	.084	.052	.043	.036
60	-.117	.105	.061	.285	.101	.059	.050	.042
61	-.263	-.029	.050	.005	.061	.068	.058	.042
62	-.253	-.036	.050	-.012	.062	.078	.068	.049
63	-.244	-.052	.049	-.042	.063	-.014	.067	.058
64	-.235	-.091	.049	-.058	.034	-.015	.066	.069
65	-.227	-.104	.049	-.079	.069	-.017	.063	.083
66	-.280	-.131	-.091	-.174	-.074	-.085	-.037	-.074
67	-.275	-.164	-.093	-.267	-.076	-.083	-.040	-.074
68	-.271	-.175	-.096	-.255	-.078	-.082	-.042	-.074
69	-.267	-.181	-.099	-.246	-.080	-.081	-.046	-.074
70	-.263	-.203	-.102	-.244	-.083	-.080	-.049	-.074

a. Plans with early or normal retirement supplements are excluded.

Table A.7
Dispersion of Accrual Rates for Table 4.3 Plans With Age 55
Early Retirement and Age 65 Normal Retirement

	Weighted Average Accrual Ratios	Median Accrual Ratios	Minimum Accrual Ratios	Maximum Accrual Ratios	Lowest 5th Percentile	Largest 5th Percentile
No. of Plans	106	106	106	106	106	106
Age						
40	.070	.073	0	.260	0	.157
41	.012	.013	0	.045	0	.027
42	.013	.015	0	.050	0	.030
43	.015	.016	0	.057	0	.034
44	.017	.018	0	.064	0	.038
45	.019	.021	0	.072	0	.043
46	.022	.024	0	.081	0	.049
47	.025	.027	0	.091	0	.055
48	.029	.031	0	.102	0	.062
49	.032	.035	0	.115	0	.071
50	.037	.039	0	.130	0	.080
51	.042	.045	0	.147	0	.092
52	.048	.041	0	.166	0	.104
53	.054	.058	0	.187	0	.119
54	.062	.067	0	.212	0	.137
55	.073	.077	0	.240	.006	.157
56	.052	.053	−.006	.195	0	.123
57	.056	.055	−.007	.192	0	.121
58	.058	.055	−.010	.189	0	.125
59	.060	.055	−.013	.183	−.008	.146
60	.061	.056	−.031	.184	−.024	.173
61	.050	.042	−.217	.204	−.051	.137
62	.050	.040	−.213	.226	−.066	.148
63	.049	.035	−.209	.400	−.082	.162
64	.049	.034	−.204	.561	−.093	.169
65	.049	.029	−.198	.328	−.101	.184
66	−.091	−.067	−.560	0	−.275	0
67	−.093	−.073	−.552	.008	−.291	0
68	−.096	−.079	−.545	.055	−.287	0
69	−.099	−.096	−.536	.045	−.283	0
70	−.102	−.101	−.528	.035	−.286	0

Table A.8
Loss in Expected Pension Wealth if Change to No-Pension Job, as Percent of Expected Wages, by Age of Job Change and by Normal Retirement Age, Starting Initial Job at Age 31

Normal Ret.	55	60	62	65
No. of Plans	184	446	442	858
Age				
31	.072	.055	.048	.026
32	.076	.058	.050	.027
33	.080	.061	.053	.028
34	.084	.064	.055	.029
35	.089	.067	.058	.030
36	.095	.071	.060	.032
37	.101	.075	.064	.033
38	.108	.079	.067	.035
39	.116	.084	.071	.037
40	.106	.083	.069	.035
41	.111	.087	.072	.037
42	.116	.092	.075	.038
43	.122	.097	.078	.040
44	.128	.103	.081	.041
45	.134	.108	.083	.043
46	.140	.115	.086	.044
47	.145	.121	.089	.046
48	.151	.128	.092	.047
49	.156	.135	.094	.048
50	.161	.143	.095	.049
51	.163	.152	.097	.050
52	.163	.161	.097	.050
53	.154	.171	.096	.050
54	.124	.182	.093	.048
55		.182	.082	.044
56		.174	.080	.043
57		.199	.077	.042
58		.237	.071	.040
59		.310	.062	.037
60			.031	.032
61			.022	.030
62				.026
63				.023
64				.016
65				

Table A.9
Loss in Expected Pension Wealth if Change to No-Pension Job,
as Percent of Expected Wages, by Age of Job Change and by
Normal Retirement Age, Starting Initial Job at Age 41

Normal Ret.	55	60	62	65
No. of Plans	57	349	546	1009
Age				
41	.079	.064	.062	.034
42	.086	.068	.066	.036
43	.093	.073	.071	.038
44	.103	079	.076	.040
45	.114	.085	.082	.043
46	.127	.092	.088	.046
47	.143	.101	.096	.050
48	.164	.111	.104	.054
49	.191	.122	.114	.058
50	.117	.096	.097	.048
51	.121	.100	.102	.049
52	.122	.103	.106	.051
53	.119	.106	.110	.052
54	.103	.108	.115	.053
55		.104	.111	.052
56		.105	.106	.053
57		.105	.111	.053
58		.100	.119	.052
59		.085	.130	.051
60			.132	.047
61			.168	.046
62				.044
63				.040
64				.031
65				

Table A.10
Loss in Expected Pension Wealth if Change to No-Pension Job, as Percent of Expected Wages, by Age of Job Change and by Normal Retirement Age, Starting Initial Job at Age 51

Normal Ret.	55	60	62	65
No. of Plans	32	178	451	1287
Age				
51	.000	.080	.094	.046
52	.000	.091	.105	.051
53	.000	.104	.118	.056
54	.000	.122	.134	.062
55		.146	.150	.069
56		.178	.169	.079
57		.229	.203	.090
58		.313	.251	.104
59		.482	.325	.122
60			.183	.059
61			.246	.060
62				.059
63				.055
64				.044
65				

Table A.11

Weighted Average Accrual Rates for Percent of Earnings Plans With 10-year Cliff Vesting, by Early and Normal Retirement Age, Starting Job at Age 41[a]

Early Ret.	55	55	55	60	60	62	62	65
Normal Ret.	55	60	65	60	65	62	65	65
No. of Plans	38	63	576	169	86	27	10	56
Age								
50	.618	.347	.209	.349	.127	.017	.135	.126
51	.106	.066	.040	.065	.026	.051	.021	.029
52	.123	.082	.046	.075	.029	.059	.024	.033
53	.141	.095	.052	.085	.035	.068	.027	.038
54	.160	.109	.060	.098	.041	.083	.030	.044
55	.184	.125	.070	.112	.047	.095	.034	.052
56	.006	.094	.069	.128	.055	.101	.037	.061
57	.002	.099	.065	.146	.064	.118	.042	.070
58	.0003	.107	.068	.167	.077	.137	.047	.085
59	−.004	.116	.071	.185	.088	.155	.053	.099
60	−.010	.120	.073	.209	.103	.179	.056	.116
61	−.016	.001	.075	−.007	.080	.198	.061	.123
62	−.022	−.004	.074	−.015	.081	.223	.067	.138
63	−.029	−.006	.075	−.023	.080	−.016	.035	.161
64	−.036	−.012	.075	−.031	.083	−.027	.034	.181
65	−.043	−.019	.073	−.040	.084	−.038	.032	.204
66	−.116	−.115	−.107	−.192	−.060	−.193	−.077	−.117
67	−.128	−.137	−.117	−.195	−.074	−.191	−.077	−.126
68	−.141	−.159	−.125	−.197	−.089	−.190	−.076	−.134
69	−.154	−.167	−.134	−.197	−.102	−.189	−.075	−.141
70	−.166	−.174	−.142	−.198	−.114	−.188	−.074	−.148

a. Plans with early or normal retirement supplements are excluded.

Table A.12
**Weighted Average Accrual Rates for Percent of Earnings Plans
With 10-Year Cliff Vesting, by Early and Normal Retirement
Age, Starting Job at Age 51[a]**

Early Ret.	55	55	55	60	60	62	62	65
Normal Ret.	55	60	65	60	65	62	65	65
No. of Plans	23	23	143	60	419	52	11	425
Age								
55	.000	0	.001	.0002	.000	.004	0	.000
56	.000	0	.001	.0002	.000	.004	0	.000
57	.000	0	.001	.0002	.000	.004	0	.000
58	.000	0	.001	.0002	.000	.003	0	.000
59	.000	0	.001	.0002	.000	.003	0	.000
60	.923	.774	.613	1.040	.451	.644	.541	.449
61	.041	.033	.081	.034	.056	.132	.091	.084
62	.036	.029	.081	.028	.059	.169	.103	.098
63	.028	.023	.082	.021	.063	.047	.077	.112
64	.022	.018	.084	.015	.065	.039	.079	.126
65	.013	.012	.081	.007	.067	.030	.083	.145
66	−.104	−.045	−.076	−.039	−.036	−.057	−.075	−.070
67	−.108	−.059	−.083	−.052	−.043	−.061	−.074	−.077
68	−.113	−.073	−.091	−.066	−.050	−.066	−.079	−.085
69	−.118	−.077	−.099	−.074	−.051	−.068	−.083	−.092
70	−.124	−.080	−.106	−.081	−.056	−.076	−.088	−.099

a. Plans with early or normal retirement supplements are excluded.

Table A.13

Weighted Average Accrual Rates for Percent of Earnings Plans With 10-Year Cliff Vesting and Early Retirement at 55, by Industry and Normal Retirement Age[a]

	Manufacturing			Transportation			Retail Trade			Finance			Services		
Early Ret.	55	55	55	55	55	55	55	55	55	55	55	55	55	55	55
Normal Ret.	55	62	65	55	62	65	55	62	65	55	62	65	55	62	65
No. of Plans	22	107	256	120	37	37	2	6	90	2	18	70	3	3	33
Age															
40	.227	.091	.056	.257	.168	.122	.021	.001	.080	.068	.086	.077	.251	.179	.068
41	.039	.019	.011	.048	.035	.021	.020	.001	.014	.027	.020	.017	.047	.033	.013
42	.045	.024	.013	.055	.040	.024	.019	.001	.0126	.033	.023	.020	.053	.037	.015
43	.051	.028	.015	.062	.045	.027	.018	.001	.017	.039	.026	.023	.060	.042	.017
44	.058	.032	.017	.070	.050	.030	.017	.002	.019	.048	.031	.026	.068	.048	.019
45	.066	.037	.020	.079	.075	.034	.015	.002	.021	.057	.035	.030	.076	.054	.023
46	.078	.041	.023	.090	.067	.035	.016	.002	.023	.068	.041	.033	.086	.061	.027
47	.089	.050	.026	.101	.075	.040	.016	.003	.026	.080	.047	.038	.098	.069	.030
48	.101	.060	.030	.114	.085	.045	.016	.003	.028	.095	.054	.044	.110	.078	.034
49	.115	.073	.035	.129	.096	.052	.087	.007	.031	.109	.067	.050	.124	.087	.041
50	.129	.080	.041	.146	.110	.060	.110	.015	.035	.130	.117	.058	.140	.099	.048
51	.146	.092	.046	.165	.127	.067	.125	.020	.038	.152	.135	.066	.157	.111	.056
52	.165	.103	.052	.187	.147	.081	.140	.022	.043	.203	.172	.092	.178	.126	.064

128

Table A.13 Continued

	Manufacturing			Transportation			Retail Trade			Finance			Services		
Early Ret.	55	55	55	55	55	55	55	55	55	55	55	55	55	55	55
Normal Ret.	55	62	65	55	62	65	55	62	65	55	62	65	55	62	65
No. of Plans	22	107	256	120	37	37	2	6	90	2	18	70	3	3	33
Age															
53	.187	.119	.063	.211	.178	.098	.163	.025	.046	.230	.193	.104	.200	.142	.075
54	.211	.134	.074	.238	.201	.111	.172	.080	.050	.267	.220	.122	.226	.160	.086
55	.240	.158	.087	.269	.228	.127	.196	.098	.056	.306	.250	.146	.254	.182	.098
56	-.008	.100	.067	-.003	.078	.091	-.182	.087	.034	.092	.141	.092	-.010	.162	.082
57	-.178	.099	.072	-.011	.093	.094	-.176	.084	.032	.083	.140	.096	-.018	.161	.087
58	-.025	.103	.079	-.019	.126	.100	-.171	.114	.027	.083	.143	.104	-.027	.158	.096
59	-.035	.102	.081	-.028	.126	.103	-.167	.107	.018	.074	.140	.108	-.035	.153	.106
60	-.046	.098	.084	-.036	.125	.109	-.164	.097	.018	.064	.134	.110	-.045	.1248	.112
61	-.057	.096	.074	-.045	.098	.093	-.161	.070	.013	-.052	.054	.099	-.053	.277	.080
62	-.068	.101	.074	-.054	.087	.086	-.159	.045	.002	-.065	.044	.098	-.062	.367	.075
63	-.079	-.080	.071	-.062	-.077	.063	-.158	-.040	-.017	-.078	-.093	.097	-.072	-.075	.069
64	-.088	-.087	.070	-.071	-.085	.062	-.159	-.054	-.027	-.088	-.100	.098	-.081	-.086	.063
65	-.099	-.095	.068	-.080	-.094	.058	-.106	-.068	-.059	-.099	-.108	.096	-.090	-.096	.054
66	-.288	-.158	-.141	-.300	-.242	-.206	-.040	-.160	-.156	-.150	-.187	-.167	-.316	-.406	-.144
67	-.288	-.174	-.152	-.301	-.276	-.217	-.044	-.158	-.158	-.206	-.214	-.175	-.311	-.400	-.152
68	-.288	-.189	-.161	-.302	-.309	-.227	-.048	-.157	-.160	-.256	-.238	-.192	-.807	-.395	-.158
69	-.288	-.204	-.170	-.302	-.320	-.237	-.045	-.158	-.161	-.300	-.245	-.207	-.302	-.390	-.164
70	-.288	-.216	-.177	-.302	-.329	-.246	-.050	-.159	-.162	-.339	-.251	-.222	-.297	-.384	-.169

a. Plans with early or normal retirement supplements are excluded.

Table A.14
Weighted Average Accrual Rates for Percent of Earnings Plans With
10-Year Cliff Vesting and Early Retirement at Age 55, by Normal
Retirement Age and Occupation[a]

Normal Ret.	55			62			65		
Occupation	Prof.	Cler.	Prod.	Prof.	Cler.	Prod.	Prof.	Cler.	Prod.
No. of Plans	53	51	48	75	74	38	204	199	110
Age									
40	.251	.240	.242	.091	.111	.115	.072	.077	.062
41	.047	.046	.044	.020	.023	.024	.015	.014	.011
42	.054	.052	.050	.026	.027	.028	.017	.017	.013
43	.061	.059	.056	.030	.031	.032	.019	.019	.016
44	.069	.066	.064	.035	.036	.036	.022	.022	.018
45	.078	.075	.073	.044	.044	.047	.025	.025	.020
46	.092	.084	.082	.045	.048	.047	.029	.028	.022
47	.105	.095	.093	.054	.057	.053	.036	.033	.025
48	.119	.107	.106	.062	.067	.063	.039	.036	.028
49	.135	.122	.120	.071	.078	.078	.045	.042	.033
50	.154	.137	.135	.086	.095	.089	.053	.048	.037
51	.175	.154	.153	.100	.108	.103	.060	.055	.041
52	.199	.175	.173	.116	.128	.117	.072	.068	.046
53	.226	.196	.196	.132	.147	.141	.083	.077	.055
54	.256	.220	.222	.155	.166	.160	.098	.089	.063
55	.291	.248	.252	.177	.191	.187	.112	.104	.075
56	.020	−.025	−.005	.102	.113	.093	.079	.070	.058
57	.012	−.036	−.012	.106	.115	.096	.082	.074	.060
58	.006	−.046	−.020	.116	.127	.112	.086	.080	.064
59	−.001	−.058	−.027	.119	.126	.109	.087	.081	.065
60	−.010	−.070	−.035	.118	.121	.104	.084	.082	.072
61	−.019	−.087	−.044	.103	.098	.097	.069	.072	.064
62	−.027	−.101	−.052	.100	.098	.096	.062	.067	.063
63	−.036	−.114	−.060	−.069	−.077	−.068	.053	.060	.055
64	−.042	−.128	−.068	−.074	−.087	−.074	.051	.052	.054
65	−.049	−.140	−.075	−.080	−.098	−.083	.038	.042	.052
66	−.295	−.295	−.290	−.171	−.203	−.199	−.167	−.157	−.133
67	−.298	−.298	−.289	−.185	−.223	−.224	−.175	−.169	−.143
68	−.303	−.300	−.288	−.199	−.242	−.247	−.184	−.180	−.149
69	−.306	−.302	−.287	−.206	−.252	−.260	−.193	−.190	−.156
70	−.310	−.304	−.286	−.214	−.261	−.272	−.201	−.199	−.160

a. Plans with early or normal retirement supplements are excluded.

Table A.15
Weighted Average Accrual Rates for Percent of Earnings Plans With 10-Year Cliff Vesting and Early Retirement at Age 55, by Normal Retirement Age and Occupation, for Manufacturing[a]

Normal Ret.	55			62			65		
Occupation	Prof.	Cler.	Prod.	Prof.	Cler.	Prod.	Prof.	Cler.	Prod.
No. of Plans	9	7	6	44	45	18	101	99	56
Age									
40	.247	.213	.219	.082	.081	.108	.064	.059	.050
41	.045	.037	.036	.018	.080	.022	.013	.009	.010
42	.051	.043	.042	.026	.021	.025	.016	.011	.012
43	.057	.049	.048	.030	.024	.028	.018	.012	.014
44	.064	.056	.054	.035	.028	.032	.021	.015	.015
45	.072	.065	.063	.040	.032	.036	.024	.017	.018
46	.091	.075	.071	.041	.039	.041	.029	.020	.020
47	.106	.085	.081	.053	.049	.046	.035	.023	.023
48	.120	.096	.091	.060	.061	.059	.040	.028	.026
49	.137	.109	.103	.068	.071	.078	.046	.034	.030
50	.155	.123	.116	.078	.077	.086	.055	.040	.034
51	.175	.139	.132	.089	.088	.099	.063	.047	.037
52	.198	.158	.148	.100	.100	.110	.072	.053	.040
53	.224	.180	.167	.114	.116	.126	.084	.064	.050
54	.253	.202	.188	.130	.131	.142	.102	.073	.058
55	.287	.231	.216	.148	.155	.172	.117	.087	.070
56	.003	.002	−.018	.089	.113	.099	.085	.071	.055
57	−.008	−.006	−.027	.088	.120	.093	.087	.084	.057
58	−.015	−.012	−.034	.093	.128	.093	.093	.095	.062
59	−.027	−.020	−.044	.095	.127	.087	.093	.102	.064
60	−.039	−.028	−.055	.094	.126	.077	.091	.107	.068
61	−.051	−.036	−.066	.092	.126	.076	.080	.101	.059
62	−.062	−.045	−.077	.097	.139	.072	.077	.099	.061
63	−.076	−.053	−.089	−.084	−.047	−.104	.070	.101	.057
64	−.081	−.062	−.100	−.088	−.053	−.113	.064	.098	.059
65	−.092	−.070	−.111	−.094	−.061	−.124	.057	.095	.060
66	−.295	−.280	−.286	−.142	−.148	−.176	−.176	−.151	−.114
67	−.304	−.276	−.282	−.151	−.176	−.198	−.182	−.166	−.127
68	−.314	−.272	−.278	−.161	−.193	−.217	−.194	−.179	−.133
69	−.323	−.270	−.273	−.171	−.211	−.235	−.203	−.189	−.141
70	−.329	−.268	−.270	−.179	−.224	−.250	−.212	−.198	−.146

a. Plans with early or normal retirement supplements are excluded.

Table A.16
Accrual in Pension Wealth by Year of Birth and Year of Hire for Managers

Year															
Born	1960	1950		1940			1930				1920				
Hired	1980	1980	1975	1980	1975	1970	1980	1975	1970	1960	1980	1975	1970	1960	1950
1980	0	0	0	0	0	508	0	0	835	2686	0	0	1178	5146	7442
1981	0	0	0	0	0	380	0	0	562	2059	0	0	-616	-105	-9132
1982	0	0	0	0	0	770	0	0	1413	3716	0	0	451	2175	-5043
1983	0	0	0	0	0	582	0	0	1079	2710	0	0	-2739	-2721	-13235
1984	0	0	1278	0	0	1494	0	2968	3053	6530	0	5090	658	3575	-2995
1985	0	0	251	0	475	767	0	18226	26481	72527	0	-5357	-5328	-8152	-14936
1986	0	0	663	0	1335	2090	0	5616	8227	13781	0	0	8151	3728	831
1987	0	0	353	0	651	994	0	2593	3691	4118	0	0	2108	-4957	-10017
1988	0	0	663	0	1289	1978	22194	4105	5874	8553	0	4176	3987	-1882	-6347
1989	1008	2158	767	4037	9	2323	831	3745	5342	5263	0	5038	2968	-3049	-7920
1990	194	388	890	688	1709	2676	1060	3280	4726	5382	0	4265	2109	-3889	-8984
1991	341	690	1051	1297	2174	3168	609	1685	2376	-7118	0	0	0	0	0
1992	418	845	1260	1601	2675	3820	-89	1389	2029	-7356	0	0	0	0	0
1993	504	1016	1485	2021	3202	4515	-908	683	1312	-8127	0	0	0	0	0
1994	606	1220	1756	2603	3851	5351	-2067	-155	419	-8902	0	0	0	0	0
1995	716	1441	2043	29639	40727	82953	5217	-1384	-3515	-10152	0	0	0	0	0
1996	843	1695	2555	7130	9538	9898	4579	3628	-939	-5346	0	0	0	0	0
1997	987	1986	2992	7349	9672	11334	3902	2855	-1652	-6363	0	0	0	0	0
1998	1153	2422	3499	7437	9641	10665	3186	2041	-2384	-7386	0	0	0	0	0
1999	1342	2969	4085	7377	9426	7844	2423	1187	-3129	-8394	0	0	0	0	0
2000	1558	3492	3900	7140	6196	8643	0	-1882	-3874	-9344	0	0	0	0	0
2001	1807	4095	4481	4432	2198	-6178	0	0	0	2002	0	0	0	0	0
2002	2093	4790	5149	3750	1206	-7237	0	0	0	0	0	0	0	0	0
2003	2517	5587	5904	2870	-15	-8380	0	0	0	0	0	0	0	0	0
2004	3037	6502	6763	1791	4378	-9658	0	0	0	0	0	0	0	0	0

Table A.16 Continued

Year															
Born	1960	1950		1940			1930				1920				
Hired	1980	1980	1975	1980	1975	1970	1980	1975	1970	1960	1980	1975	1970	1960	1950
2005	2918	95433	117775	-2553	-8981	-11004	0	0	0	0	0	0	0	0	0
2006	3361	11955	14674	-1993	-4042	-6843	0	0	0	0	0	0	0	0	0
2007	3872	13705	16840	-2784	-4988	-7994	0	0	0	0	0	0	0	0	0
2008	4461	13022	15944	-3601	-5955	-9155	0	0	0	0	0	0	0	0	0
2009	5139	9809	11879	-4436	-6930	-10299	0	0	0	0	0	0	0	0	0
2010	5910	10923	13211	-5265	-7875	-11375	0	0	0	0	0	0	0	0	0
2011	6792	-6583	-8668	0	0	0	0	0	0	0	0	0	0	0	0
2012	7801	-7785	-10184	0	0	0	0	0	0	0	0	0	0	0	0
2013	8940	-9069	-11809	0	0	0	0	0	0	0	0	0	0	0	0
2014	10223	-10418	-13531	0	0	0	0	0	0	0	0	0	0	0	0
2015	168439	11848	-15345	0	0	0	0	0	0	0	0	0	0	0	0
2016	21859	-868	-12662	0	0	0	0	0	0	0	0	0	0	0	0
2017	25137	-9994	-14317	0	0	0	0	0	0	0	0	0	0	0	0
2018	23904	-11319	-15955	0	0	0	0	0	0	0	0	0	0	0	0
2019	17968	-12627	-17524	0	0	0	0	0	0	0	0	0	0	0	0
2020	19964	-13849	-18933	0	0	0	0	0	0	0	0	0	0	0	0
2021	-12355	0	0	0	0	0	0	0	0	0	0	0	0	0	0
2022	-14649	0	0	0	0	0	0	0	0	0	0	0	0	0	0
2023	-17087	0	0	0	0	0	0	0	0	0	0	0	0	0	0
2024	-19659	0	0	0	0	0	0	0	0	0	0	0	0	0	0
2025	-22287	0	0	0	0	0	0	0	0	0	0	0	0	0	0
2026	-21570	0	0	0	0	0	0	0	0	0	0	0	0	0	0
2027	-24026	0	0	0	0	0	0	0	0	0	0	0	0	0	0
2028	-26391	0	0	0	0	0	0	0	0	0	0	0	0	0	0
2029	-28576	0	0	0	0	0	0	0	0	0	0	0	0	0	0
2030	-30436	0	0	0	0	0	0	0	0	0	0	0	0	0	0

Table A.17
Pension Wealth by Year of Birth and Year of Hire for Managers

Year → Born / Hired ↓	1960	1950		1940			1930				1920				
Hired →	1980	1980	1975	1980	1975	1970	1980	1975	1970	1960	1980	1975	1970	1960	1950
1980	0	0	0	0	0	2356	0	0	3747	17190	0	0	20270	69954	157647
1981	0	0	0	0	0	2741	0	0	4313	19221	0	0	19347	68974	145742
1982	0	0	0	0	0	3654	0	0	5969	23790	0	0	20361	73204	144173
1983	0	0	0	0	0	4493	0	0	7480	28076	0	0	18515	74336	137819
1984	0	0	1393	0	2692	6327	0	3235	1149	475	0	5549	20077	81625	140844
1985	0	0	1740	0	3350	7494	0	23271	40597	117141	0	0	15322	77017	131943
1986	0	0	2513	0	4901	9985	0	30051	50713	135785	0	0	24639	83260	136584
1987	0	0	2969	0	5750	11351	0	33728	56172	144117	0	0	27634	80214	129531
1988	0	0	3775	0	7317	13828	0	39157	64165	157520	0	4552	32763	80434	126280
1989	1098	2352	4718	4400	9136	16751	24192	44347	71802	167710	0	10173	36925	79385	121217
1990	1341	2842	5821	5274	11257	20142	25781	49175	78983	178316	0	15109	40267	77390	114850
1991	1750	3675	7132	6837	13946	24166	27668	52407	83814	175617	0	0	0	0	0
1992	2256	4700	8707	8776	17257	29015	29115	55404	88399	172570	0	0	0	0	0
1993	2869	5940	10572	11227	21234	34755	29840	57713	92326	168587	0	0	0	0	0
1994	3610	7439	12785	14382	26033	41572	29695	59178	95397	163658	0	0	0	0	0
1995	4493	9220	15373	47095	71162	133166	28282	59343	94264	157222	0	0	0	0	0
1996	5539	11329	18594	56201	83574	147728	34770	64980	95910	155849	0	0	0	0	0
1997	6772	13814	22381	65802	96481	164262	40746	69931	96824	153324	0	0	0	0	0
1998	8220	16844	26827	75768	109717	180531	46151	74133	96962	149607	0	0	0	0	0
1999	9915	20558	32040	85956	123101	194197	50931	77527	96299	144698	0	0	0	0	0
2000	11894	24946	37197	96169	133336	209110	55012	77669	94800	138605	0	0	0	0	0
2001	14201	30116	43135	103721	139506	208294	0	0	0	0	0	0	0	0	0
2002	16884	36190	49968	110745	144770	206303	0	0	0	0	0	0	0	0	0
2003	20105	43304	57817	117006	148850	203005	0	0	0	0	0	0	0	0	0
2004	23984	51616	66824	122269	157833	198220	0	0	0	0	0	0	0	0	0

Table A.17 Continued

Year	1960	1950		1940			1930				1920				
Born / Hired	1980	1980	1975	1980	1975	1970	1980	1975	1970	1960	1980	1975	1970	1960	1950
2005	27844	157100	197093	122952	152517	191845	0	0	0	0	0	0	0	0	0
2006	32295	174574	218662	124257	152424	189811	0	0	0	0	0	0	0	0	0
2007	37429	194452	243204	124738	151301	186468	0	0	0	0	0	0	0	0	0
2008	43351	214150	267468	124345	149092	181767	0	0	0	0	0	0	0	0	0
2009	50180	230907	287992	123032	145761	175690	0	0	0	0	0	0	0	0	0
2010	58041	249344	310538	120773	141301	168260	0	0	0	0	0	0	0	0	0
2011	67087	249226	309879	0	0	0	0	0	0	0	0	0	0	0	0
2012	77489	247793	307546	0	0	0	0	0	0	0	0	0	0	0	0
2013	89425	244918	303375	0	0	0	0	0	0	0	0	0	0	0	0
2014	103100	240494	297212	0	0	0	0	0	0	0	0	0	0	0	0
2015	289618	234391	288904	0	0	0	0	0	0	0	0	0	0	0	0
2016	321636	231555	283275	0	0	0	0	0	0	0	0	0	0	0	0
2017	358138	227214	275686	0	0	0	0	0	0	0	0	0	0	0	0
2018	394330	221307	266097	0	0	0	0	0	0	0	0	0	0	0	0
2019	425077	213809	254529	0	0	0	0	0	0	0	0	0	0	0	0
2020	458866	204763	241094	0	0	0	0	0	0	0	0	0	0	0	0
2021	458390	0	0	0	0	0	0	0	0	0	0	0	0	0	0
2022	455392	0	0	0	0	0	0	0	0	0	0	0	0	0	0
2023	449660	0	0	0	0	0	0	0	0	0	0	0	0	0	0
2024	440956	0	0	0	0	0	0	0	0	0	0	0	0	0	0
2025	429144	0	0	0	0	0	0	0	0	0	0	0	0	0	0
2026	417780	0	0	0	0	0	0	0	0	0	0	0	0	0	0
2027	403414	0	0	0	0	0	0	0	0	0	0	0	0	0	0
2028	386063	0	0	0	0	0	0	0	0	0	0	0	0	0	0
2029	365842	0	0	0	0	0	0	0	0	0	0	0	0	0	0
2030	343022	0	0	0	0	0	0	0	0	0	0	0	0	0	0

Table A.18
Social Security Accrual by Year of Birth and Year of Hire for Managers

Year Born:	1960	1950		1940			1930				1920				
Hired	1980	1980	1975	1980	1975	1970	1980	1975	1970	1960	1980	1975	1970	1960	1950
1980	0	1696	2286	398	455	467	936	982	1022	1071	2936	3000	3057	3125	1263
1981	0	235	338	474	567	635	1121	1240	1291	1356	3726	3808	3880	2013	4053
1982	0	289	421	571	676	742	1346	1462	1524	802	4460	4557	4644	4843	4878
1983	0	364	522	730	863	954	1730	1893	1978	2137	5850	5982	3317	6383	6431
1984	0	293	390	588	273	734	1394	1489	1525	1673	4893	4974	5206	5332	5361
1985	0	129	382	612	767	760	1471	1578	1611	1777	5023	1436	5307	5483	5510
1986	0	419	440	751	910	919	1822	1949	2003	2200	-5991	-5837	-6118	-6463	-6540
1987	0	520	560	971	1165	1199	2385	2577	1232	2914	-5587	-5443	-5706	-6028	-6100
1988	0	588	608	1098	1294	1334	2725	2930	3129	3313	-5208	-5074	-5319	-5618	-5686
1989		664	664	1242	1441	1488	3117	3338	3566	3774	-4856	-4731	-4959	-5238	-5301
1990	3965	737	729	1404	1609	1663	3568	3810	4072	4308	-4530	-4413	-4627	-4887	-4945
1991	358	801	804	690	1801	1863	4090	2095	4661	4929	0	0	0	0	0
1992	382	875	889	1865	2022	2092	4696	5103	5349	5653	0	0	0	0	0
1993	416	961	985	2096	2273	2353	5402	5878	6158	6504	0	0	0	0	0
1994	456	1060	1093	2361	2562	2653	6330	6815	7169	7589	0	0	0	0	0
1995	503	1173	1216	2665	2892	2994	6924	7376	7801	8257	0	0	0	0	0
1996	556	1301	1355	3015	3271	3387	-6909	-7275	-7825	-8497	0	0	0	0	0
1997	616	1448	1512	3418	3709	3839	-6444	-6784	-7298	-7925	0	0	0	0	0
1998	683	1614	1689	3885	4213	4361	-6006	-6324	-6802	-7387	0	0	0	0	0
1999	758	1803	1891	4426	4797	4965	-5600	-5896	-6343	-6888	0	0	0	0	0
2000	841	2018	2119	5052	5472	5662	-5224	-5501	-5917	-6425	0	0	0	0	0
2001	935	2263	2378	5779	6256	6471	0	0	0	0	0	0	0	0	0
2002	1040	2542	2674	6628	7169	7413	0	0	0	0	0	0	0	0	0
2003	1158	2861	3010	7624	8241	8518	0	0	0	0	0	0	0	0	0
2004	1291	3225	3394	8900	9648	9986	0	0	0	0	0	0	0	0	0

Table A.18 Continued

Year Born Hired	1920 1950	1960	1970	1975	1980	1930 1960	1970	1975	1980	1940 1970	1975	1980	1950 1975	1980	1960 1980
2005	0	0	0	0	0	0	0	0	0	10863	10496	9684	3832	3641	1440
2006	0	0	0	0	0	0	0	0	0	-11747	-11207	-10010	4334	4119	1607
2007	0	0	0	0	0	0	0	0	0	-10956	-10452	-9335	4912	4668	1796
2008	0	0	0	0	0	0	0	0	0	-10212	-9743	-870	5578	5302	2009
2009	0	0	0	0	0	0	0	0	0	-9522	-9085	-8114	6346	6034	2251
2010	0	0	0	0	0	0	0	0	0	-8883	-8475	-7569	7232	6878	2524
2011	0	0	0	0	0	0	0	0	0	0	0	0	8259	7858	2834
2012	0	0	0	0	0	0	0	0	0	0	0	0	9454	8999	3188
2013	0	0	0	0	0	0	0	0	0	0	0	0	10855	10337	3590
2014	0	0	0	0	0	0	0	0	0	0	0	0	12766	12137	4049
2015	0	0	0	0	0	0	0	0	0	0	0	0	13885	13201	4571
2016	0	0	0	0	0	0	0	0	0	0	0	0	-15516	-14510	5169
2017	0	0	0	0	0	0	0	0	0	0	0	0	-14471	-13532	5858
2018	0	0	0	0	0	0	0	0	0	0	0	0	-13489	-12614	6651
2019	0	0	0	0	0	0	0	0	0	0	0	0	-12577	-11761	7566
2020	0	0	0	0	0	0	0	0	0	0	0	0	-11733	-10972	8622
2021	0	0	0	0	0	0	0	0	0	0	0	0	0	0	9844
2022	0	0	0	0	0	0	0	0	0	0	0	0	0	0	11265
2023	0	0	0	0	0	0	0	0	0	0	0	0	0	0	12933
2024	0	0	0	0	0	0	0	0	0	0	0	0	0	0	15222
2025	0	0	0	0	0	0	0	0	0	0	0	0	0	0	16557
2026	0	0	0	0	0	0	0	0	0	0	0	0	0	0	-18659
2027	0	0	0	0	0	0	0	0	0	0	0	0	0	0	-17401
2028	0	0	0	0	0	0	0	0	0	0	0	0	0	0	-1622
2029	0	0	0	0	0	0	0	0	0	0	0	0	0	0	-15124
2030	0	0	0	0	0	0	0	0	0	0	0	0	0	0	-14109

Table A.19
Social Security Wealth by Year of Birth and Year of Hire for Managers

Year Born →	1960	1950		1940			1930				1920				
Hired \ Year	1980	1980	1975	1980	1975	1970	1980	1975	1970	1960	1980	1975	1970	1960	1950
1980	0	1849	2491	3818	4854	5277	9217	10544	11703	13137	30795	32286	33612	35218	33536
1981	0	2082	2828	4287	5412	5905	10325	11765	12966	14452	34476	36037	37425	36976	37540
1982	0	2453	3364	5025	6295	6873	12070	13676	14977	15716	40267	41976	43496	43251	43869
1983	0	2988	4121	6102	7588	8297	14633	16505	17971	18925	48898	50847	49546	52631	53335
1984	0	3444	4734	7021	8232	9476	16820	18881	20454	21613	56463	58589	57482	60844	61612
1985	0	3765	5398	8055	9499	10801	19305	21590	23281	24682	64896	63223	66278	70009	70846
1986	0	4328	6031	9101	10760	12109	21837	24326	26123	27779	60203	58651	61485	64946	65722
1987	0	5017	6811	10417	12334	13759	25054	27823	28206	31742	55816	54377	57005	60214	60934
1988	0	5800	7667	11909	14094	15603	28734	31804	32415	36252	51720	50387	52821	55795	56462
1989	0	6689	8607	13599	16062	17666	32944	36342	37218	41390	47889	46654	48909	51662	52280
1990	4321	7681	9645	15514	18270	19978	37764	41522	42708	47255	44305	43162	45248	47796	48367
1991	4834	8771	10795	16706	20752	22576	43294	44984	49000	53969	0	0	0	0	0
1992	5387	9973	12069	19213	23543	25495	49638	51820	56218	61658	0	0	0	0	0
1993	5992	11303	13484	22040	26686	28780	56928	59691	64518	70489	0	0	0	0	0
1994	6659	12778	15058	25238	30235	32487	65441	68810	74160	80757	0	0	0	0	0
1995	7396	14418	16809	28856	34242	36670	74839	78796	84760	92041	0	0	0	0	0
1996	8212	16245	18762	32960	38778	41400	69429	73099	78632	85387	0	0	0	0	0
1997	9115	18283	20941	37618	43918	46757	64370	67773	72903	79166	0	0	0	0	0
1998	10117	20559	23375	42917	49752	52832	59643	62796	67549	73352	0	0	0	0	0
1999	11230	23107	26098	48957	56391	59741	55229	58149	62550	67923	0	0	0	0	0
2000	12464	25960	29145	55848	63950	67602	51096	53798	57869	62841	0	0	0	0	0
2001	13836	29161	32562	63728	72579	76568	0	0	0	0	0	0	0	0	0
2002	15362	32758	36398	72757	82448	86815	0	0	0	0	0	0	0	0	0
2003	17059	36803	40709	83126	93763	98557	0	0	0	0	0	0	0	0	0
2004	18948	41360	45561	95178	106932	112229	0	0	0	0	0	0	0	0	0

Table A.19 Continued

Year (Hired)	Born 1960 / 1980	Born 1950 / 1980	Born 1950 / 1975	Born 1940 / 1980	Born 1940 / 1975	Born 1940 / 1970	Born 1930 / 1980	Born 1930 / 1975	Born 1930 / 1970	Born 1930 / 1960	Born 1920 / 1980	Born 1920 / 1975	Born 1920 / 1970	Born 1920 / 1960	Born 1920 / 1950
2005	21054	46502	51030	108431	121404	127251	0	0	0	0	0	0	0	0	0
2006	23402	52306	57197	100587	112621	118045	0	0	0	0	0	0	0	0	0
2007	26021	58874	64169	93258	104415	109444	0	0	0	0	0	0	0	0	0
2008	28948	66320	72065	86413	96751	101410	0	0	0	0	0	0	0	0	0
2009	32222	74775	81023	80016	89589	93904	0	0	0	0	0	0	0	0	0
2010	35884	84387	91198	74029	82886	86877	0	0	0	0	0	0	0	0	0
2011	39989	95342	102782	0	0	0	0	0	0	0	0	0	0	0	0
2012	44595	107848	115995	0	0	0	0	0	0	0	0	0	0	0	0
2013	49770	122167	131108	0	0	0	0	0	0	0	0	0	0	0	0
2014	55592	138854	148734	0	0	0	0	0	0	0	0	0	0	0	0
2015	62149	157176	168081	0	0	0	0	0	0	0	0	0	0	0	0
2016	69541	145806	155922	0	0	0	0	0	0	0	0	0	0	0	0
2017	77894	135183	144562	0	0	0	0	0	0	0	0	0	0	0	0
2018	87349	125260	133950	0	0	0	0	0	0	0	0	0	0	0	0
2019	98068	115986	124033	0	0	0	0	0	0	0	0	0	0	0	0
2020	110241	107308	114753	0	0	0	0	0	0	0	0	0	0	0	0
2021	124092	0	0	0	0	0	0	0	0	0	0	0	0	0	0
2022	139882	0	0	0	0	0	0	0	0	0	0	0	0	0	0
2023	157939	0	0	0	0	0	0	0	0	0	0	0	0	0	0
2024	179001	0	0	0	0	0	0	0	0	0	0	0	0	0	0
2025	202114	0	0	0	0	0	0	0	0	0	0	0	0	0	0
2026	187497	0	0	0	0	0	0	0	0	0	0	0	0	0	0
2027	173836	0	0	0	0	0	0	0	0	0	0	0	0	0	0
2028	161075	0	0	0	0	0	0	0	0	0	0	0	0	0	0
2029	149149	0	0	0	0	0	0	0	0	0	0	0	0	0	0
2030	137991	0	0	0	0	0	0	0	0	0	0	0	0	0	0

Table A.20
Wage Earnings by Year of Birth and Year of Hire for Managers

Year Born	1960	1950		1940			1930				1920				
Hired	1980	1980	1975	1980	1975	1970	1980	1975	1970	1960	1980	1975	1970	1960	1950
1980	20405	24053	33021	27894	34020	40712	31825	34945	38666	48446	35723	35788	36519	40186	47598
1981	22852	26082	34967	29403	35354	41853	32739	35666	39226	48813	36005	35902	36470	39794	46774
1982	25312	28057	36807	30819	36586	42898	33548	36289	39693	49098	36188	35919	36323	39280	45765
1983	27757	29965	38542	32141	37720	43858	34256	36819	40074	49300	36275	35845	36080	38642	44568
1984	30615	32271	40774	33869	39342	45410	35390	37818	40977	50156	36813	36215	36277	38446	43828
1985	33479	34543	42948	35535	40904	46913	36447	38741	41803	50919	37271	36488	36362	38092	42847
1986	36331	36774	45069	37140	42409	48374	37427	39588	42551	51579	37632	36660	36333	37574	41624
1987	39155	38960	47139	38685	43859	49794	38331	40358	43216	52122	37900	36728	36181	36885	40157
1988	41933	41092	49158	40163	45250	51168	39152	41042	43785	52524	38066	36679	35895	36014	38445
1989	44653	43166	51128	41572	46580	52493	39886	41633	44249	52765	38124	36507	35467	34956	36499
1990	47309	45183	53056	42913	47850	53766	40530	42127	44599	52826	38067	36205	34891	33713	34339
1991	49904	47147	54951	44187	49059	54987	41083	42517	44827	52690	0	0	0	0	0
1992	52429	49052	56809	45387	50198	56140	41533	42790	44914	52329	0	0	0	0	0
1993	54889	50900	58636	46509	51262	57216	41873	42935	44847	51724	0	0	0	0	0
1994	57292	52698	60438	47553	52247	58206	42099	42946	44616	50861	0	0	0	0	0
1995	59645	54444	62216	48514	53142	59093	42200	42809	44207	49725	0	0	0	0	0
1996	61954	56140	63969	49382	53935	59860	42166	42513	43607	48307	0	0	0	0	0
1997	64230	57786	65695	50151	54615	60487	41988	42048	42805	46602	0	0	0	0	0
1998	66481	59380	67389	50812	55166	60954	41656	41403	41794	44615	0	0	0	0	0
1999	68717	60920	69047	51353	55573	61236	41161	40570	40568	42359	0	0	0	0	0
2000	70946	62398	70655	51760	55816	61307	40493	39542	39125	39852	0	0	0	0	0
2001	73178	63814	72206	52023	55879	61148	0	0	0	0	0	0	0	0	0
2002	75415	65151	73676	52123	55739	60728	0	0	0	0	0	0	0	0	0
2003	77667	66402	75052	52047	55381	60028	0	0	0	0	0	0	0	0	0
2004	79931	67550	76307	51779	54783	59027	0	0	0	0	0	0	0	0	0

Table A.20 Continued

Year	1960	1950		1940			1930				1920				
Born															
Hired	1980	1980	1975	1980	1975	1970	1980	1975	1970	1960	1980	1975	1970	1960	1950
2005	82213	68581	77417	51305	53931	57709	0	0	0	0	0	0	0	0	0
2006	84502	69471	78349	50609	52810	56063	0	0	0	0	0	0	0	0	0
2007	86796	70199	79069	49678	51410	54084	0	0	0	0	0	0	0	0	0
2008	89081	70739	79543	48503	49727	51778	0	0	0	0	0	0	0	0	0
2009	91347	71067	79735	47081	47764	49160	0	0	0	0	0	0	0	0	0
2010	93567	71151	79604	45408	45526	46251	0	0	0	0	0	0	0	0	0
2011	95721	70965	79114	0	0	0	0	0	0	0	0	0	0	0	0
2012	97774	70478	78230	0	0	0	0	0	0	0	0	0	0	0	0
2013	99694	69665	76922	0	0	0	0	0	0	0	0	0	0	0	0
2014	101438	68503	75168	0	0	0	0	0	0	0	0	0	0	0	0
2015	102959	66974	72952	0	0	0	0	0	0	0	0	0	0	0	0
2016	104202	65062	70267	0	0	0	0	0	0	0	0	0	0	0	0
2017	105115	62766	67124	0	0	0	0	0	0	0	0	0	0	0	0
2018	105638	60090	63546	0	0	0	0	0	0	0	0	0	0	0	0
2019	105712	57051	59572	0	0	0	0	0	0	0	0	0	0	0	0
2020	105277	53675	55254	0	0	0	0	0	0	0	0	0	0	0	0
2021	104279	0	0	0	0	0	0	0	0	0	0	0	0	0	0
2022	102671	0	0	0	0	0	0	0	0	0	0	0	0	0	0
2023	100415	0	0	0	0	0	0	0	0	0	0	0	0	0	0
2024	97484	0	0	0	0	0	0	0	0	0	0	0	0	0	0
2025	93875	0	0	0	0	0	0	0	0	0	0	0	0	0	0
2026	89598	0	0	0	0	0	0	0	0	0	0	0	0	0	0
2027	84690	0	0	0	0	0	0	0	0	0	0	0	0	0	0
2028	79209	0	0	0	0	0	0	0	0	0	0	0	0	0	0
2029	73239	0	0	0	0	0	0	0	0	0	0	0	0	0	0
2030	66886	0	0	0	0	0	0	0	0	0	0	0	0	0	0

Table A.21
Cumulated Earnings by Year of Birth and Year of Hire for Managers

Year — Born	1960	1950		1940			1930				1920				
Hired	1980	1980	1975	1980	1975	1970	1980	1975	1970	1960	1980	1975	1970	1960	1950
1980	20405	24053	33021	27894	34020	40712	31825	34945	38666	48446	35723	35788	36519	40186	47598
1981	43257	50135	67987	57297	69374	82565	64564	70611	77892	97258	71728	71690	72990	79980	94372
1982	68569	78192	104795	86116	105960	125463	98112	106900	117585	146356	107916	107609	109312	119259	140137
1983	96326	108157	143337	120257	143679	169320	132368	143719	157659	195656	144193	143453	145392	157901	184704
1984	126941	140428	184111	154126	183022	214730	167758	181537	198636	245812	181012	179669	181669	196348	228532
1985	160419	174970	227059	189661	223926	261644	204205	220277	240439	296731	218283	216157	218031	234440	271379
1986	196750	211745	272127	226801	266335	310017	241631	259865	282989	348310	255915	252817	254364	272014	313003
1987	235905	250750	319267	265486	310194	359811	279962	300224	326205	400432	293815	289545	290545	308900	353159
1988	277838	291797	368425	305649	355444	410979	319114	341266	369990	452956	331881	326224	326440	344913	391604
1989	322490	334963	419553	347221	402025	463472	359000	382899	414239	505721	370005	362731	361907	379870	428104
1990	369799	380146	472609	390134	449874	517238	399530	425026	458838	558547	408072	398936	396799	413582	462442
1991	419703	427293	527560	434321	498933	572225	440613	467543	503665	611237	0	0	0	0	0
1992	472132	476345	584369	479708	549132	628365	482147	510333	548579	663567	0	0	0	0	0
1993	527021	527245	643004	526216	600394	685581	524020	553268	593426	715290	0	0	0	0	0
1994	584313	579942	703442	573770	652640	743787	566118	596214	638043	766151	0	0	0	0	0
1995	643958	634387	765658	622283	705782	802880	608318	639024	682250	815877	0	0	0	0	0
1996	705913	690527	829626	671666	759717	862740	650484	681537	725857	864183	0	0	0	0	0
1997	770143	748313	895321	721817	814332	923228	692472	723585	768662	910785	0	0	0	0	0
1998	836623	807692	962710	772629	869498	984181	734128	764987	810456	955400	0	0	0	0	0
1999	905341	868612	1031757	823981	925071	1045417	775289	805557	851024	997759	0	0	0	0	0
2000	976286	931010	1102412	875741	980887	1106724	815782	845099	890149	1037610	0	0	0	0	0
2001	1049464	994824	1174617	927764	1036766	1167871	0	0	0	0	0	0	0	0	0
2002	1124879	1059974	1248293	979886	1092505	1228598	0	0	0	0	0	0	0	0	0
2003	1202545	1126376	1323345	1031934	1147885	1288626	0	0	0	0	0	0	0	0	0
2004	1282476	1193926	1399652	1083712	1202667	1347652	0	0	0	0	0	0	0	0	0

Table A.21 Continued

Year

Born	1960	1950		1940			1930				1920				
Hired	1980	1980	1975	1980	1975	1970	1980	1975	1970	1960	1980	1975	1970	1960	1950
2005	1364688	1262507	1477069	1135017	1256598	1405361	0	0	0	0	0	0	0	0	0
2006	1449190	1331987	1555417	1185625	1309408	1461423	0	0	0	0	0	0	0	0	0
2007	1535985	1402176	1634486	1235302	1360818	1515506	0	0	0	0	0	0	0	0	0
2008	1625066	1472915	1714028	1283805	1410544	1567283	0	0	0	0	0	0	0	0	0
2009	1716412	1543982	1793763	1330886	1458307	1616442	0	0	0	0	0	0	0	0	0
2010	1809979	1615133	1873366	1376293	1503833	1662692	0	0	0	0	0	0	0	0	0
2011	1905700	1686097	1952480	0	0	0	0	0	0	0	0	0	0	0	0
2012	2003474	1756574	2030709	0	0	0	0	0	0	0	0	0	0	0	0
2013	2103168	1826239	2107631	0	0	0	0	0	0	0	0	0	0	0	0
2014	2204605	1894742	2182799	0	0	0	0	0	0	0	0	0	0	0	0
2015	2307564	1961716	2255750	0	0	0	0	0	0	0	0	0	0	0	0
2016	2411765	2026778	2326016	0	0	0	0	0	0	0	0	0	0	0	0
2017	2516879	2089544	2393140	0	0	0	0	0	0	0	0	0	0	0	0
2018	2622516	2149634	2456686	0	0	0	0	0	0	0	0	0	0	0	0
2019	2728227	2206684	2516257	0	0	0	0	0	0	0	0	0	0	0	0
2020	2833503	2260359	2571510	0	0	0	0	0	0	0	0	0	0	0	0
2021	2937782	0	0	0	0	0	0	0	0	0	0	0	0	0	0
2022	3040452	0	0	0	0	0	0	0	0	0	0	0	0	0	0
2023	3140866	0	0	0	0	0	0	0	0	0	0	0	0	0	0
2024	3238350	0	0	0	0	0	0	0	0	0	0	0	0	0	0
2025	3332224	0	0	0	0	0	0	0	0	0	0	0	0	0	0
2026	3421822	0	0	0	0	0	0	0	0	0	0	0	0	0	0
2027	3506511	0	0	0	0	0	0	0	0	0	0	0	0	0	0
2028	3585719	0	0	0	0	0	0	0	0	0	0	0	0	0	0
2029	3658958	0	0	0	0	0	0	0	0	0	0	0	0	0	0
2030	3725843	0	0	0	0	0	0	0	0	0	0	0	0	0	0

Table A.22
Calculation of Pension Benefits and Wealth Accrual

Year	Age	Yrs. Svc.	Wage	Avg. earn. base	Normal Ret. Ben.	SS	SS Adjmt.	Adj. Ret. Ben. Factor	Early Ret. Reduct. Ben.	Reduced Normal Ret. Ben.
(1)	(2)	(3)	(4)	(5)	(6)	(7)	(8)	(9)	(10)	(11)
1979	49	20	32393	24788	9915	10227	3846	6069	1.00	9915
80	50	21	37109	27501	11550	10626	4276	7274	1.00	11550
81	51	22	41266	29221	12857	10921	4673	8185	1.00	12857
82	52	23	44055	32165	14796	11060	5000	9796	1.00	14796
83	53	24	45661	33664	16159	11128	5293	10866	1.00	16159
84	54	25	48426	38018	19009	11248	5620	13388	1.00	19009
1985	55	26	50919	39451	20120	11341	5937	14183	0.67	13480
86	56	27	54674	44313	23043	11528	6316	16727	0.73	16821
87	57	28	58564	45896	24325	11719	6707	17618	0.80	19460
88	58	29	62556	49248	26594	11911	7107	19487	0.87	23137
89	59	30	66616	52526	28890	12099	7513	21377	0.93	26867
1990	60	31	70697	55797	31246	12289	7929	23317	1.00	31246
91	61	32	74741	59206	33747	12475	8352	25395	1.00	33747
92	62	33	78682	62875	36468	12658	8781	27687	1.00	36468
93	63	34	82443	66655	39326	12848	9223	30103	1.00	39326
94	64	35	85930	70545	42327	13047	9682	32645	1.00	42327
1995	65	36	89053	74365	45362	13264	10164	35198	1.00	45362
96	66	37	91700	78046	48389	13757	10575	37814	1.00	48389
97	67	38	93772	81515	51354	14273	11005	40349	1.00	51354
98	68	39	95164	84687	54200	14813	11455	42745	1.00	54200
99	69	40	95769	87473	56857	15377	11926	44932	1.00	56857
2000	70	41	95509	89780	59255	15972	12421	46834	1.00	59255

Table A.22 (Continued)

Reduced Adjusted Ret. Ben.	Annuity Value	Prob. Survive To 65	Discount 65 To Current Age	Present Value Ret. Ben. From 65	Present Value Ret. Ben. To 65	Pension Wealth	Pension Accrual	Pension Accrual/ Wage	Age
(12)	(13)	(14)	(15)	(16)	(17)	(18)	(19)	(20)	(21)
6069	7.999	0.8196	0.2519	10023	0	10023	0	0.0	49
7274	7.999	0.8243	0.2745	13167	0	13167	2057	6.4	50
8185	7.999	0.8294	0.2993	16250	0	16250	1741	4.7	51
9796	7.999	0.8351	0.3262	21346	0	21346	3334	8.1	52
10866	7.999	0.8415	0.3555	26004	0	26004	2510	5.7	53
13388	7.999	0.8485	0.3875	35216	0	35216	6205	13.8	54
9503	7.999	0.8562	0.4224	27494	89947	117441	72527	149.8	55
12210	7.999	0.8648	0.4604	38891	105041	143932	14607	28.7	56
14095	7.999	0.8742	0.5019	49468	112461	161930	4627	8.5	57
16954	7.999	0.8847	0.5470	65637	121970	187606	10187	17.4	58
19880	7.999	0.8963	0.5963	84994	126740	211734	6645	10.6	59
23317	7.999	0.9092	0.6499	110219	128422	238640	7202	10.8	60
25395	7.999	0.9235	0.7084	132909	116203	249112	-10097	-14.3	61
27687	7.999	0.9395	0.7722	160676	98801	259477	-11060	-14.8	62
30103	7.999	0.9574	0.8417	194046	74665	268711	-12953	-16.5	63
32645	7.999	0.9774	0.9174	234174	42327	276501	-15040	-18.2	64
35198	7.999	1.0000	1.0000	281568	0	281568	-18181	-21.2	65
37814	7.824	1.0000	1.0000	295848	0	295848	-10148	-11.4	66
40349	7.646	1.0000	1.0000	308518	0	308518	-12804	-14.0	67
42745	7.466	1.0000	1.0000	319112	0	319112	-15754	-16.8	68
44932	7.281	1.0000	1.0000	327147	0	327147	-18978	-19.9	69
46834	7.093	1.0000	1.0000	332181	0	332181	-22394	-23.4	70

Table A.23
Earnings Parameter Estimates by Employee Group
(1980 $)[a]

Variable	Employee Group				
	Managers	Salesmen	Saleswomen	Male Office Workers	Female Office Workers
Constant	9.28 (122.2)	8.87 (303.6)	8.65 (7.0)	5.80 (210.9)	8.39 (826.6)
A	0.021 (4.8)	0.037 (23.5)	0.042 (7.0)	0.16 (83.3)	0.45 (71.6)
A2	-.000082 (-1.4)	-.00041 (-20.7)	-.00051 (-6.5)	-.0019 (-77.2)	-.00057 (-66.3)
A2S	0.000021 (3.0)	0.000064 (19.7)	-0.000047 (-2.0)	0.000044 (12.9)	0.000029 (20.1)
S	0.18 (14.0)	0.20 (31.5)	-0.036 (-0.9)	0.10 (17.5)	0.10 (48.7)
S2	-0.01 (-7.8)	-0.0044 (-11.5)	-0.0086 (-2.9)	-0.0060 (-13.8)	-0.0031 (-24.4)
S2A	0.00020 (7.5)	0.00017 (11.9)	0.00023 (1.8)	0.00018 (15.7)	0.00010 (21.5)
AS	-0.0043 (-7.1)	-0.0068 (-23.8)	0.0040 (2.0)	-0.0033 (-11.5)	-0.0030 (-26.3)
A2S2	-0.0000016 (-6.5)	-0.0000017 (-12.7)	-0.0000016 (-1.2)	-0.0000016 (-15.7)	-9.035 (-19.5)

Table A.23, Continued

Variable		Employee Group			
	Managers	Salesmen	Saleswomen	Male Office Workers	Female Office Workers
1969	0.11 (9.4)	0.15 (31.4)	-0.027 (-0.6)	0.031 (3.8)	0.039 (11.2)
1970	0.16 (14.1)	0.19 (38.8)	-0.014 (-0.3)	0.063 (7.8)	0.058 (17.5)
1971	0.19 (17.2)	0.19 (39.6)	0.0036 (0.1)	0.062 (8.0)	0.036 (11.5)
1972	0.21 (19.1)	0.21 (45.6)	-0.012 (-0.3)	0.088 (11.6)	0.065 (21.3)
1973	0.21 (19.3)	0.21 (46.3)	0.0027 (0.1)	0.094 (12.8)	0.076 (25.7)
1974	0.16 (15.2)	0.20 (44.3)	-0.0074 (-0.2)	0.079 (11.0)	0.069 (24.6)
1975	0.10 (9.7)	0.14 (31.6)	-0.012 (-0.4)	0.071 (10.2)	0.049 (18.0)
1976	0.15 (14.2)	0.16 (36.0)	0.042 (1.6)	0.12 (17.5)	0.11 (41.1)
1977	0.14 (13.6)	0.16 (36.1)	0.094 (4.2)	0.10 (15.4)	0.084 (33.6)

Table A.23

Earnings Parameter Estimates by Employee Group

(1980 $)[a]

	Employee Group				
Variable	Managers	Salesmen	Saleswomen	Male Office Workers	Female Office Workers
Constant	9.28 (122.2)	8.87 (303.6)	8.65 (7.0)	6.80 (210.9)	8.39 (826.6)
A	0.021 (4.8)	0.037 (23.5)	0.042 (7.0)	0.16 (83.3)	0.45 (71.6)
A2	-.000082 (-1.4)	-0.00041 (-20.7)	-0.00051 (-6.5)	-0.0019 (-77.2)	-0.00057 (-66.3)
A2S	0.000021 (3.0)	0.000064 (19.7)	-0.000047 (-2.0)	0.000044 (12.9)	0.000029 (20.1)
S	0.18 (14.0)	0.20 (31.5)	-0.036 (-0.9)	0.10 (17.5)	0.10 (48.7)
S2	-0.01 (-7.8)	-0.0044 (-11.5)	-0.0086 (-2.9)	-0.0060 (-19.8)	-0.0031 (-24.4)
S2A	0.00020 (7.5)	0.00017 (11.9)	0.00023 (1.8)	0.00018 (16.7)	0.00010 (21.5)
AS	-0.0043 (-7.1)	-0.0068 (-23.8)	0.0040 (2.0)	-0.0033 (-11.5)	-0.0030 (-26.3)
A2S2	-0.0000016 (-6.5)	-0.0000017 (-12.7)	-0.0000016 (-1.2)	-0.0000016 (-15.7)	-9.035 (-19.5)

Table A.23, Continued

			Employee Group		
Variable	Managers	Salesmen	Saleswomen	Male Office Workers	Female Office Workers
1969	0.11 (9.4)	0.15 (31.4)	-0.027 (-0.6)	0.031 (3.8)	0.039 (11.2)
1970	0.16 (14.1)	0.19 (38.8)	-0.014 (-0.3)	0.063 (7.8)	0.058 (17.5)
1971	0.19 (17.2)	0.19 (39.6)	0.0036 (0.1)	0.062 (8.0)	0.036 (11.5)
1972	0.21 (19.1)	0.21 (45.6)	-0.012 (-0.3)	0.088 (11.6)	0.065 (21.3)
1973	0.21 (19.3)	0.21 (46.3)	0.0027 (0.1)	0.094 (12.8)	0.076 (25.7)
1974	0.16 (15.2)	0.20 (44.3)	-0.0074 (-0.2)	0.079 (11.0)	0.069 (24.6)
1975	0.10 (9.7)	0.14 (31.6)	-0.012 (-0.4)	0.071 (10.2)	0.049 (18.0)
1976	0.15 (14.2)	0.16 (36.0)	0.042 (1.6)	0.12 (17.5)	0.11 (41.1)
1977	0.14 (13.6)	0.16 (36.1)	0.094 (4.2)	0.10 (15.4)	0.384 (33.5)

Table A.23, Continued

			Employee Group		
Variable	Managers	Salesmen	Saleswomen	Male Office Workers	Female Office Workers
1978	0.18 (17.7)	0.18 (41.9)	0.13 (6.7)	0.09 (14.3)	0.078 (32.3)
1979	0.13 (13.5)	0.10 (24.6)	0.064 (3.7)	0.058 (9.0)	0.044 (18.8)
1980	—	—	—	—	—
1981	0.03 (3.0)	0.0091 (2.1)	0.025 (1.5)	0.021 (3.3)	0.013 (5.6)
1982	-0.0086 (-0.9)	-0.077 (-18.0)	-0.033 (-2.1)	0.033 (5.1)	0.012 (5.1)
1983	0.0028 (-0.3)	-0.099 (-23.0)	-0.041 (-2.6)	0.073 (11.3)	0.066 (28.4)
1984	0.068 (7.0)	-0.11 (-25.2)	-0.050 (-3.3)	0.0078 (1.2)	0.032 (13.8)
σ^2_ε	0.135	0.155	0.163	0.168	0.065
σ^2_υ					
σ^2_η					

a. t-statistics are in parentheses.

REFERENCES

Aaron, Henry J. 1982. *Economic Effects of Social Security.* Washington, D.C.: Brookings Institution.

Allen, Steven G., Robert L. Clark, and Ann A. McDermed. 1987a. "Why Do Pensions Reduce Mobility?" Mimeographed. North Carolina State University.

Allen, Steven G., Robert L. Clark, and Ann A. McDermed. 1987b. "Pension Wealth, Age-Wealth Profiles, and the Distribution of Net Worth." Working Paper. Raleigh: North Carolina State University.

Blinder, Alan. 1982. "Private Pensions and Public Pensions: Theory and Fact," NBER Working Paper No. 902 (June).

Blinder, Alan, and Roger Gordon. 1980. "Market Wages, Reservation Wages and Retirement," *Journal of Public Economics* 14: 277-308.

Blinder, Alan, Roger Gordon, and Donald Wise. 1980. "Reconsidering the Work Disincentive Effects of Social Security," *National Tax Journal* 33 (December): 431-42.

Blinder, Alan, Roger Gordon, and Donald Wise. 1981. "Life Cycle Savings and Bequests: Cross-Sectional Estimates of the Life Cycle Model." NBER Working Paper No. 619 (January).

Boskin, Michael. 1977. "Social Security and Retirement Decisions," *Economic Inquiry* 15 (January): 1-25.

Boskin, Michael, and Michael Hurd. 1978. "The Effect of Social Security on Early Retirement," *Journal of Public Economics* 10 (December): 361-77.

Bulow, J. 1979. "Analysis of Pension Funding Under ERISA." NBER Working Paper No. 402.

Burkhauser, Richard V. 1977. "An Asset Maximization Approach to Early Social Security Acceptance." Discussion Paper 463-77. Institute for Research on Poverty.

Burkhauser, Richard V., and Joseph P. Quinn. 1983. "Inferring Retirement Behavior: Key Issues for Social Security," *Journal of Policy Analysis and Management* 3, 1 (Fall): 1-13.

Burkhauser, Richard V., and John A. Turner. 1978. "A Time-Series Analysis on Social Security and its Effect on the Market Work of Men at Younger Ages," *Journal of Political Economy* (August).

Burkhauser, Richard V., and John Turner. 1981. "Can Twenty Five Million Americans Be Wrong?—A Response to Blinder, Gordon and Wise." *National Tax Journal* 34 (December): 467-72.

Burtless, Gary. 1986. "Social Security, Unanticipated Benefit Increases, and the Timing of Retirement." *Review of Economic Studies* 53 (October): 781-805.

Burtless, Gary, and J. Hausman. 1978. " 'Double Dipping': The Combined Effects of Social Security and Civil Service Pensions on Employee Retirement," *Journal of Political Economics* 18: 139-160.

Burtless, Gary, and Robert A. Moffitt. 1984. "The Effects of Social Security On The Labor Supply of The Aged," in Henry Aaron and Gary Burtless, eds., *Retirement and Economic Behavior*. Washington, D.C.: Brookings Institution, 135-74.

Burtless, Gary, and Robert Moffitt. 1986. "Social Security, the Earnings Test, and the Age at Retirement," *Public Finance Quarterly* 14: 3-27.

Campbell, C.D., and R.G. Campbell. 1976. "Conflicting Views on the Effect of Old-Age and Survivors' Insurance on Retirement," *Economic Inquiry* 14 (September): 369-88.

Clark, Robert L., and Stephen A. Gohmann. 1982. "Retirement and the Acceptance of Social Security Benefits." Mimeographed. Raleigh: North Carolina State University.

Clark, Robert L., and Ann A. McDermed. 1987. "Pension Wealth and Job Changes: The Effects of Vesting Portability and Lump-Sum Distributions." Working Paper. North Carolina State University.

Crawford, V., and D. Lilien. 1981. "Social Security and the Retirement Decision," *Quarterly Journal of Economics* 96 (August): 509-29.

Diamond, P., and J. Hausman. 1984. "The Retirement and Unemployment Behavior of Older Men," in H. Aaron and G. Burtless, eds., *Retirement and Economic Behavior*. Washington, D.C.: Brookings Institution.

Fields, Gary S., and Olivia Mitchell. 1982. "The Effects of Pensions and Earnings on Retirement: A Review Essay," in R. Ehrenberg, ed., *Research in Labor Economics* 5: 115-156.

Fields, Gary S., and Olivia Mitchell. 1983. "Economic Incentives to Retire: A Qualitative Choice Approach." NBER Working Paper No. 1096.

Fields, Gary S., and Olivia Mitchell. 1984a. "Economic Determinants of the Optimal Retirement Age: An Empirical Investigation," *Journal of Human Resources* 19 (Spring): 245-62.

Fields, Gary S., and Olivia Mitchell. 1984b. "The Economics of Retirement Behavior," *Journal of Labor Economics* 2 (January): 84-105.

Fields, Gary S., and Olivia Mitchell. 1985. *Retirement, Pensions, and Social Security*. Cambridge, MA: MIT Press.

Gustman, Alan, and Thomas L. Steinmeier. 1983. "Minimum Hours and Retirement Behavior," *Contemporary Policy Issues*, 3.

Gustman, Alan, and Thomas Steinmeier. 1986a. "A Disaggregate Structural Analysis of Retirement," *Review of Economics and Statistics*, 68, 3 (August).

Gustman, Alan, and Thomas Steinmeier. 1986a. "A Structural Retirement Model," *Econometrica*, 54, 3 (May).

Gustman, Alan, and Thomas Steinmeier. 1985. "Social Security Reform and Labor Supply," *Journal of Labor Economics* 3, 2 (April).

Hausman, J. and David Wise. 1985. "Social Security, Health Status, and Retirement," in David Wise, ed., *Pensions, Labor and Individual Choice*. Chicago: University of Chicago Press.

Hurd, Michael and Michael Boskin. 1984. "The Effect of Social Security on Retirement in the Early 1970s." *Quarterly Journal of Economics* (November): 767-790.

Irelan, L. 1976. "Retirement History Study: Introduction," in U.S. Department of Health, Education and Welfare, Social Security Administration, Office of Research and Statistics, *Almost 65: Baseline Data from the Retirement History Study*. Washington, D.C.: GPO.

Kotlikoff, Laurence J. 1978. "Social Security, Time for Reform," in *Federal Tax Reform: Myth or Reality*. San Francisco: Institute for Contemporary Studies.

Kotlikoff, Laurence J., and Daniel Smith. 1983. *Pensions in the American Economy*. Chicago: University of Chicago Press.

Kotlikoff, Laurence J., and David A. Wise. 1985. "Labor Compensation and the Structure of Private Pension Plans: Evidence for Contractual versus Spot Labor Markets," in David Wise, ed., *Pensions, Labor, and Individual Choice*. Chicago: University of Chicago Press.

Kotlikoff, Laurence J., and David A. Wise. 1987. "The Incentive Effects of Private Pension Plans," in Zvi Bodie, John Shoven, and David Wise, eds., *Issues in Pension Economics*. Chicago: University of Chicago Press.

Kotlikoff, Laurence J., and David A. Wise. 1988. "Employee Retirement and a Firm's Pension Plan," in David Wise, eds., *Economics of Aging*. Chicago: University of Chicago Press.

Lazear, E.P. 1981. "Severance Pay, Pensions, Mobility, and the Efficiency of Work Incentives." Mimeographed, University of Chicago.

Lazear, E.P. 1983. "Pensions as Severance Pay," in Zvi Bodie and John B. Shoven, eds., *Financial Aspects of the United States Pension System*. Chicago: University of Chicago Press.

Parsons, Donald O. 1980. "The Decline in Male Labor Force Participation," *Journal of Political Economy* 88 (February): 117-134.

Pellechio, Anthony J. 1978. "The Social Security Earnings Test, Labor Supply Distortions, and Foregone Payroll Tax Revenue." NBER Working Paper No. 272 (August).

Quinn, Joseph P. 1977. "Microeconomic Determinants of Early Retirement: A Cross-Sectional View of White Married Men," *Journal of Human Resources* 12, 3 (Summer): 329-46.

Ransom, Roger L., and Richard Sutch. 1986. "The Labor of Older Americans: Retirement of Men On and Off the Job, 1870-1937," *Journal of Economic History* 61, 1 (March).

INDEX

Accounting procedures: for pension accrual, 2-3; *See also* Accrual ratio; Actuarial calculations

Accrual rate profile, 16; at differing ages, 23-25; with differing plans, 42-43; with early retirement less than actuarial reduction, 18-19; effect of interest rate changes on, 20-22; in FIRM, 78-83; FIRM variation by employee type, 86-88; FIRM variation in, 83-86; with flat benefits, 51-54; fluctuation in, 37-43; and mechanisms to limit mobility, 98; with retirement supplements, 48-52; sensitivity to early retirement provisions, 26

Accrual ratios, 51-52, 63-67, 68, 70, 72-73

Actuarial calculations: effect of discount factor, 15-16, 101; of increments, 104

Age Discrimination Act of 1986, 19, 39

Age patterns: age-accrual profiles, 101; age-earnings estimates, 107-113; age-earnings profiles, 11-12, 140; age-marginal productivity profile, 11-12; age-tenure profile, 35-37; age-wage profile, 30-35; determinants under vested accrual, 9; effect for pension accrual of, 2

Backloading: definition and effect of, 1-2; intent of ERISA and Tax Reform 1986 to limit, 2, 9; possible effect of, 98-99; presumed effect of ERISA in limiting, 88; in standard defined benefit plan, 15-16

Benefit loss: FIRM, 86-83; if changing to no-pension job, 57-63

Benefits availability, 89, 91

Blinder, Alan, 6, 7

BLS-LOB. *See* Bureau of Labor Statistics 1979 Level of Benefits Survey (BLS-LOB)

Boskin, Michael, 6, 7, 98

Budget constraint, 91-92

Bulow, Jeremy, 100n.2

Bureau of Labor Statistics 1979 Level of Benefits Survey (BLS-LOB), 3, 29-30

Burkhauser, Richard V., 7

Burtless, Gary, 6, 7, 98

Cliff vesting, 11, 16-17, 23, 37, 40

Compensation: decline in total, 40; loss under FIRM pension plan, 80-83, 95-96; to obtain continued service with FIRM, 84-85; pension benefit accrual conditions to raise, 97; reduction in, 40-42; relation between wages and pension benefits as, 12

Contract market theory, 1, 2, 10-12, 98

CPS. *See* Current Population Survey (CPS)

Current Population Survey (CPS), 4

Data sources, 3-4

Departure rates: by age in FIRM, 92, 95; correlated with availability of social security benefits, 91, 92; correlated with FIRM early retirement benefits, 89, 91-92, 95-96; correlated with years of service in FIRM, 89, 91, 92, 95

Diamond, P., 7

Discount factor, 15-16, 101

Disincentives, 8, 26-27

153